UNLEASHING YOUR FULL POTENTIALS

(Step Into Your Supernatural Potential)

NATHANIEL KOGI SAINGBE

NAKS Publications

ISBN - 9798327794986

Published and Printed in the United States in 2024

For information on distribution or other details, please contact, Nathaniel Kogi Saingbe
nakspublications@gmail.com

DEDICATION

To the glory of God, whose grace and mercy know no abounds, I dedicate this book. With deepest gratitude, I acknowledge God's divine inspiration, guiding every word penned within these pages. His teachings illuminate the path, infusing this work with purpose and meaning.

I am profoundly grateful to my wife, who meticulously edited the manuscripts, and our children for their unwavering encouragement, inspiration, and support throughout this journey. Your love is my anchor, and your belief in my endeavors ignites my determination. I hold you all in the highest regard.

This book is dedicated to those who seek refuge and enlightenment within the sanctuary of literature, recognizing the profound impact of words on the human soul. May its pages serve as a source of solace, inspiration, and transformation. Together, let us embark on a journey of discovery as we allow the power of storytelling to provoke thought, stir emotions, and ignite imaginations. This book is a celebration of our collective journey, for your contributions are woven into the very fabric of this work. With gratitude and humility, I share this moment with you all.

ACKNOWLEDGEMENT

My appreciation goes to the Lord God Almighty, under whose protective arms I have come this far. I appreciate my wonderful parents, who invested in me and brought me up in the fear of the Lord. Thank you, Dad, for your passionate prayer always, and to my mom of blessed memory. To my DCB Connecticut Family, your prayers and support have kept my family and me going over the years. Together, we have overcome obstacles and rise above challenges. The best is yet to come! ....

TABLE OF CONTENT

CONTENTS

INTRODUCTION

THE BREATH OF GOD IS IN YOU

Recognizing your potential is crucial for your journey in life. It is like having a treasure box within you, filled with unique gifts and abilities that set you apart from everyone else. God, in His infinite wisdom, crafted you with a purpose, endowing you with potentials designed to propel you toward greatness. Picture your potentials as keys to unlocking doors of opportunities, creativity, and fulfillment. Just like a seed holds the potential to grow into a mighty tree, your abilities have the power to blossom into something extraordinary. It's like having a toolbox filled with tools; each potential is a tool waiting for you to pick up and use to shape your life and impact the world around you. It is true that life's challenges or the fear of failure might cause you to doubt these potentials within you, but you must remember that the fear of failure can stagnate your growth.

Think about Joseph from the Bible, for instance, He had the potential to interpret dreams, and although life wasn't really fair to him, he didn't let his circumstances or setbacks bury his gift. Instead, he stayed with it and kept pruning it, when the time came, his ability led him to a position of influence and honor. Just like Joseph, when you recognize and nurture your potential, you position yourself for a future filled with purpose and success.

You also have to know that your potentials aren't just for personal gain; they're meant to impact the world positively. Whether it's a talent for music, a knack for problem-solving, or a gift for leadership, your abilities are meant to be shared. When you unleash these potentials, you don't just elevate your life; you become a beacon of hope and inspiration to those around you-so, believe in yourself. Trust in the divine abilities God has bestowed upon you. As you explore and unleash your potential, you will find yourself on a journey toward self-discovery, growth, and making a great impact in the world around you.

Many people do not realize what they have and who they are, but the truth is that you were not born empty. Into your soul was breathed irreplaceable gifts, seeds of greatness, and a divine imprint longing to be unleashed. The very same Spirit that raised Jesus from the dead, the breath of life that hovered over the waters at creation, dwells in the innermost chamber of your being and this means that you hold within you every talent and ability needed to fulfill your purpose and live a great life on earth.

Though the voice of fear may try convincing you otherwise, whispering to you that you lack what is required to do great things in life, it is certain that when God made you, He left nothing out. You are not missing anything, in fact, you have direct access to unlimited inner resources. Right now, you might be thinking, *how could that be possible for me? My life often feels ordinary and small. I wrestle with doubts, make mistakes, and face the same headaches as everyone else.* But I want you to know that accepting your greatness begins with remembering just how miraculous it is that you have to be here at all. Out of infinite probabilities, you were chosen to receive the gift of life.

This introductory invitation is but the first step on an exciting journey of awakening to your fullest divine potentials...

All scriptures are taken from the King James version of the Bible, except otherwise stated.

SECTION 1

YOU ARE LOADED WITH POTENTIALS

CHAPTER 1

UNLEASHING THE DIVINE WITHIN YOU

"Never mistake yourself for an empty vessel. You are a reservoir of God-given talents, brimming with the ability to change the world around you."

◆ ◆ ◆

Too Loaded To Be Wasted

The world today is a great place only because people realize that God has given them great potential, only because people understand that they are not empty and that they can do something to make the world a better place. If God did not create man to have potentials, then the world would never have advanced to where it is today.

God is a God of potentials, a God of countless possibilities, He is unlimited in power, that's why He is called Omnipotent, meaning He has all power, all ability, all creativity, and everything you can imagine. You cannot put God in a tight corner and as a matter of fact, you need to understand that He is the first artist that ever existed. The Bible tells us that He formed man, that is, He crafted him and designed him intentionally. And how did He do it? He created man in His own image and likeness. Genesis 1:26 says "*Then God said, let Us make man in Our image, according to Our likeness; let them have dominion over the fish of the sea, over the birds of the air, and over the cattle, over all the earth and over every creeping thing that creeps on the earth.*"

If you are made in God's image and likeness, do you realize you have His creativity, His potentials, His breadth, His life, His wisdom, and His power at work in you? Never come to the point where you feel worthless, useless, or feel like an empty vessel. God never created anything that is a waste of time. You are loaded with potentials, you are a bag of possibilities, an embodiment of God, with the potential of God stirring inside you. Hallelujah! Glory to God! You are God's handiwork. God sees the diamond in you even when you cannot see it yourself. He sees the positive possibilities in your life even when all you see is struggle and hardship. He sees the gifts and talents He has placed inside you, just waiting to be uncovered. Do not discount yourself, you have so much to offer this world. Your potential is limitless when you walk with God. You didn't come to this world as an empty vessel, you didn't come as a waste of time, you didn't come to this world as a liability, you came because God loaded you with potential to make the world a better place.

As you read this book, you must to know that there is a purpose for your life, God has plans to use you in amazing ways. You may not see it right now, but trust that God is at work and He has loaded you with enough potential to see that you accomplish the goals and purpose He created you to fulfill. He is equipping you, preparing you, and molding you into the person He wants you to be and this is exactly why He has brought this book your way. It is a great revelation to help you unravel the treasures of God's breath in you. Every experience in your life, good and bad, is being used to shape your character and strengthen you to the point where your potential will be refined. Ponder on that once more, "God does not create a waste product; you are loaded with potential."

Are you set to unleash those potentials and change the world? Then it's time to stop looking down on yourself, it's time to stop looking at the situation surrounding you, it's time to start looking inward and unraveling the mysteries and great dimensions of potential within you. Be encouraged today, lift up your eyes to the One who breathed life into you. You have barely scratched the surface of what God wants to do through you, your best is yet to come, the world is waiting for the solution that you have to offer, and God is counting on you not to let Him down. God has promised that His plans for you are good and not evil, to give you a hope and future (Jeremiah 29:11). You have not seen what He is going to do next. Just when you think you have reached your limit, God will surprise you by doing more than you could have imagined both in your life and through your life. He will open doors you never expected. He will bring the right people into your life to push you forward. He will take you places you never dreamt possible. Others may not know what mountain lies before you but it is crucial that you know that your potential in God is unlimited!

The key is to keep seeking God every day, to stay close to Him through prayer, worshiping and reading His Word, and believing that you are loaded with His potential. As you devote yourself to Him, He will keep transforming you and conforming you to His image. He will develop your gifts, ignite new passions in you, and empower you to step out in faith. Please do not lean on your own understanding, but trust in Him wholeheartedly. He knows the plans He has for you. You may feel ordinary today, but through God, you can do extraordinary things. Not by your own strength and power, but by His Spirit working mightily within you, by the potentials he placed in you by reason of His life and breadth in you. Be bold and courageous, do not shrink back. Your potential in God is astounding, so say YES to His calling. Let Him use you to impact your generation so that you can shine brightly for His glory. The world is waiting for you!

The Covering Veil:

You see, the covering veil is the reason many people do not realize how great and resourceful they are. They have been blinded from seeing their God-given potential. When you read the word of God, it is so obvious in the Bible that God did not put mankind here just to manage and survive by mere luck. Yes, and this must become settled in your heart; you must recognize this just like you know your own name -God did not put you here simply to struggle day in and day out.

In our world today, when you call somebody and ask, “How are you doing?” They will just say, "We are managing." They are not using "managing" to mean they are in charge, no, it’s completely different. As a matter of fact, the phrase "we are managing" actually means things are not fine, we are suffering, we are struggling, we are barely surviving, and life has not been fair. You have to know that this is not God's plan for you, God did not put you here just to manage. If you are merely managing something, then it means you are not at your best. If you are just managing your health, you are not at your best. If you are managing your finances, you are not at your best. If you are managing your marriage, then there is also a problem. Living in a constant state of managing conditions is not God's best for you, it is not! That kind of life is only a strategy from the devil to press and pressure you to the point where your eyes become veiled and you no longer realize the great potential of possibilities that God has placed inside of you.

The devil knows that when you continually focus on the troubles and challenges around you, you will never truly see the potentials, talents, gifts, and even spiritual resources that God has given you. The covering veil refers to the challenges, situations, and events that blind you to your true worth and what God has put inside your life. The devil does not want you to know how powerful God created you to be. But this book is meant to open your eyes and remove those scales. He knows there is so much within you, so he keeps covering your eyes and sight with the challenges of life. He wants to distract you and weigh you down so you never operate in the fullness of your identity as a child of God.

The Bible says in Mark 4:19, "And the cares of this world, the deceitfulness of riches, and the desires for other things entering in choke the word, and it becomes unfruitful." Why must you consider this scripture now? It is to let you know that even right now as you are reading this book, if care is not taken, the devil will still use your challenges, situations, bad conditions, and unpaid bills to blind you from seeing the potential of God within you. But you must refuse to allow Him. You must accept this truth that God has placed divine potentials within you! The word of Grace is coming to you today, a word that says God has gifted you tremendously and has plans to use you powerfully for His Kingdom. The enemy wants to keep that knowledge buried, the enemy wants you to think you are helpless and worthless but God is saying, “NO MORE!” It is time for you to break free from limitations and step into the destiny God has for you by recognizing that you have potentials that need to be released.

God is speaking to you and He is saying, “*See yourself as I see you, my precious child, my child filled with my supernatural power and abilities, my child filled and loaded with potential and talents. I have put dreams, visions, and promises inside of you. I have anointed you for greatness! You are stronger than you think and nothing can hold you back as you put your trust in Me*”. Beloved, it's time for the veil to be torn away! The prayer is that as you read this book, God is lifting the covering and opening your eyes. You are not weak, rather, you are mighty through Him! You are not insignificant, you are called and equipped for impact! You are not limited, neither are your potentials in God endless!

Cry out to Him today and ask God to peel back any layers and veil still obscuring your vision. Pray for an impartation of His Spirit to stir up the gifts within you, open your heart fully to receive all He has for you, and stay expectant, for your breakthrough is not far! There is a strong conviction that God has new levels of influence, favor, and authority waiting for you as you begin to recognize your potentials and the need to unleash and release them. But it starts with seeing yourself as He sees you, His Word says you are the head and not the tail, above and not beneath! You are strong in Him. His power works mightily in you. You can do all things through Christ who gives you strength! Awaken to your true identity. Your moment is now!

A Timid Lion

The word "timid" is defined in Merriam-Webster's Dictionary as "feeling or showing a lack of courage or self-confidence." Do you really think this is what God designed you to be? Of course not! God did not design you to be timid or fearful, as a matter of fact, He created you in His image, so you are meant to be bold, courageous, creative, and full of wisdom. The Bible says He has not given us a spirit of fear, but of love, of power, and of a sound mind. There is so much potential within you! Stop being a lion that is timid, you are meant to be bold and fearless in confronting life and situations.

When you read the book of Judges 6:12, the Bible records this about Gideon- “And the Angel of the Lord appeared to him, and said to him,

'The Lord *is* with you, you mighty man of valor!'" Where was Gideon? He was hiding and he was scared. He was a lion, but he did not know anything about his potential, so he could not unleash it. As you read, are you already thinking about your potentials or are you still hiding like Gideon? Gideon had the potential to save the nation, he had the potential to end their suffering but he was timid and hiding because the circumstances around him had found a way to veil his eyes from seeing what God had placed inside of him.

Are you like Gideon? Do you have difficult circumstances that caused you to hide away? Then, now is the time to stand up and fight back! It's time to unleash your true potential. It's time to show the world that you are a deliverer, not a coward. God is counting on you; you are not empty, but a mighty man and woman of valor, wisdom, grace, strength, and power. You first need to believe it before it can be unleashed. God sees your potential even when you cannot. He believes in you even when you doubt yourself. He is saying to you right now, *"Arise and shine! Do not hide your light any longer. I have gifted you and purposed you for great things. Take courage, for I am with you. I will make you strong and help you fulfill your destiny."*

Beloved, the Lion of Judah lives within you! He wants

to awaken a bold, fiery, lion-like faith on your inside. Feel Him releasing a mighty roar from your spirit, declaring, "I am not timid anymore! Through Christ, I am empowered and victorious!" Too long the enemy has overwhelmed you and made you feel weak. But not anymore! Today a supernatural confidence is rising up. You are not defined by your fears, failures, or feelings of inadequacy. You are defined by Him who dwells within you, the Lion of Judah! He is stirring up your gifts, breaking limitations, and calling you to step out.

Judges 6:14-16 says, "*And the Lord looked upon him, and said, Go in this thy might, and thou shalt save Israel from the hand of the Midianites: have not I sent thee? And he said unto him, Oh my Lord, wherewith shall I save Israel? behold, my family is poor in Manasseh, and I am the least in my father's house. And the Lord said unto him, Surely I will be with thee, and thou shalt smite the Midianites as one man.*"

Did God add anything else to Gideon? Of course not, He only said, "Go in this thy might." Do you know what this means? It means Gideon had might but didn't know it, he was a mighty man of valor but didn't know it, he was a deliverer but didn't know it, ultimately revealing that he had potentials but couldn't release them because he wasn't aware of them. Rather, what was his response? It was the response of a timid lion. He kept complaining, saying, "*Oh Lord, I am poor. Oh Lord, my family is small,*" just the way you are saying, "Oh Lord, I cannot do anything. Oh Lord, I don't have connections. Oh Lord, I don't know a politician who can help me." However, the Lord is saying to you, "*Go in this your might*! Go in your potential. Go in your strength!" There is strength within you, there is power within you. It's time to come out of timidity. It's time to look inward and begin unleashing your potential.

Gideon was a mighty man; the deliverance of the nation was in his hands but he didn't know it. You see, God has placed in you the deliverance of your family, your friends, and your nation. So, will you rise up? Or will you keep thinking you are small and helpless? Will you begin to nurture that singing potential, preaching potential, business acumen, leadership quality, and writing potential? Will you begin to look inward and stop allowing situations around you to make you timid and veil your eyes from all that God has created you to be? Beloved, the time is now to unleash the potential God has placed inside of you! No more cowering in fear. No more hiding in the shadows. God is calling you out to fulfill your destiny!

What gifts and talents has He put in you that are just

waiting to be discovered? What dreams and passions has He planted in your heart that you have not dared to pursue? Listen for His whisper urging you forward into new adventures. Feel His power rising up within you to confidently step out in faith. You were created for impact, not obscurity. You have a significant part to play in God's plan. But it starts by stopping the doubt and embracing who God says you are - His masterpiece! Ephesians 2:10 says, "For we are His workmanship, created in Christ Jesus for good works, which God prepared beforehand that we should walk in them." Yes, you are strong in Him, you are equipped by Him, and you have everything needed for a great life and to fulfill your purpose. Be encouraged today. Lift your eyes to the One who calls you mighty, His plans for you are good. He has plans to prosper you and give you hope and a future. Trust Him, obey Him, and allow Him to ignite your potential. Great adventures await as you, so boldly follow His leading! What He will do through your life will be nothing short of remarkable. Get ready for divine connections, sudden breakthroughs, and new realms of possibility. I assure you that the best of your life is yet to come, so say "YES" to His call today.

No more hiding who you are. It's time to rise

up boldly as the lion He created you to be.
Your roar is needed in this generation.

Turn your eyes upon Jesus. He will revive and empower you for all that lies ahead. Roar courageously, mighty one - your time is now! Get ready to see doors open that you never imagined possible. Expect favor and acceleration. Watch as God uses you powerfully right where you are. Your influence is expanding and your impact is amplifying. You are dangerous to the enemy because the Lion of Judah is with you, so walk boldly in your calling today and roar courageously against every opposition. It's time to live without limits because the Lion is on your side!

CHAPTER 2

UNLOCKING YOUR GOD-GIVEN POTENTIALS

"The transfer of your potentials into your life began with the breathing of the Almighty into your nostrils."

◆ ◆ ◆

When you look at Genesis 2:7, especially in the New King James Version, the Bible says, "And the Lord God formed man of the dust of the ground, and breathed into his nostrils the breath of life; and man became a living being." I want to focus on that verse. It says that God formed man out of the dust, breathed into his nostrils the breath of life, and man became a living soul. If God had stopped at just molding and forming man without breathing into him, the product would have just been an empty vessel. It would be like any one of us making a lifeless artwork, carving on a tree, or creating an image using clay.

Some artworks today are very expensive, costing millions. But they have no life in them, they are just things man has formed. But right here in the book of Genesis, the Word of God says, "After God formed man, He then breathed into him." This also means that God is the first artist ever known. God being the first artist we know from the Scripture, didn't just speak man into being. He formed him, He took dust and molded it, He shaped it with His own hands, He made the legs, feet, hands, head, eyes, everything. After shaping man, what did God then do? The figure looked human but had no life, no movement, no activity, and ultimately, absolutely no potential. Why?- because there was no breath in the product!. Then God said, now I will release myself, my strength, my abilities, my life, and my potentials into what I've made. I will breathe into him.

The key point is this, the transfer of your potential into your life began with the breathing of the Almighty into your nostrils. The moment God breathed into Adam was when potential was transferred. I know you might be tempted to say, "Ah, but that was just Adam."

No! I tell you the truth, every one of us here today has had God's breath in us. When did this happen? It started months before you were born. Nobody knows the exact day, minute, hour, or second when you began to breathe and your heart started beating in your mother's womb. But that was the moment the potentials of God were breathed into you! God imparted His divine gifts and talents into you right from conception. He put a measure of His creativity, wisdom, power, purpose, and potential inside of you. Your life is not random or accidental, you have been meticulously designed by the Master Architect, and you are full of potential and abilities.

So why do so many go through life never unlocking their potential? Why do gifts and talents lie dormant? Because the enemy wants to keep you from knowing who you truly are. His goal is to weigh you down with lies and frustrations so you never operate in your God-given power. But today, God is saying - NO MORE! It's time for you to awaken to your true identity as His workmanship! Throw off the false labels and limiting mindsets you may have carried over time. The same power that raised Jesus from the dead lives in you! God has destined you for greatness. Step into your authority as His child, unlock those gifts inside, and take hold of all He has for you! Your moment is now, the world needs to see the true, unlimited, unstoppable version of you! Say goodbye to mediocrity and being stuck in a rut. God is breathing new life and purpose into your spirit, He is reigniting your passion and accelerating your progress. Get ready for unprecedented favor and opportunity, this is your season to do what you were created for. Your potential is astounding. God's power in you is unmatched, and all that's required is your trust, obedience, and a willingness to step out - He will do the rest. He's simply looking for willing vessels to pour out His power through. You were uniquely designed by Him and for Him. So, once more, it's time to let your light shine!

Discovering Treasures in the Desert:

Your life may feel like a wilderness right now. It may seem like nothing good can come from your situation. People may have given up on you, your circumstances may appear dry and barren -but let me tell you an important truth, just because the sea looks calm on the surface doesn't mean there are no treasures hidden within. There are thousands of species living in the ocean depths, even though the surface appears quiet and empty. Gold and precious minerals are not found lying plain on the ground. Sometimes you have to dig through dirt, debris, and refuse to uncover buried treasure. In the same way, your life is filled with untapped potential, gifts, talents, and purpose. Just because you cannot see them now does not mean they are not there. God has deposited seeds of greatness within you. Even when your situation looks bleak, there are treasures waiting to be discovered.

The enemy wants to convince you that your life is worthless and insignificant. He wants you to believe the desert season you are in is meaningless. But that is a lie! God uses the desert to develop and refine you for greater things ahead. In the desert, your roots grow deeper, your character is shaped, and your trust and reliance on God increases. Remember, even Jesus was led by the Holy Spirit into the desert to be tested and prepared for ministry. It was in the dry, barren wilderness that He became empowered to fulfill His purpose. Friend, do know that you are not a barren desert, you are a fruitful land. There are treasures in you to be uncovered. A sad truth is that sometimes you must go through difficulty to discover who God has called you to be. It is when you are weary and desperate that His strength is made perfect in your weakness.

It's time to begin digging for the treasures within you

and to start uncovering your potential even in the midst of the wilderness. Shortly, you will find several powerful steps to help you begin to uncover and unlock the potentials within you.

You see, humans are truly remarkable creatures with the capacity to create amazing literature, art, and music. Mankind created vaccines that prevented millions of deaths and even created technology that has made the world a really wonderful place. He has been to the moon and back, explored the depths of the sea, and has even attempted to create human beings by cloning them. How about plants and animal hybrids? Yes, some of these things are not expressly giving God glory, but they show the limitless possibilities of our potentials and what God has empowered each of us to be able to do. Truly speaking, it appears that as a species, his potential is limitless .

However, things can feel a little different on an individual basis. This is because the majority of us are unaware of our strengths and have a hazy notion that we are capable of accomplishing some great and amazing things. However, figuring out how to even approach our own potential is difficult. So let me share with you some techniques to unleash your inner potential.

- **Live by Kingdom Values:**

Take a close look at your life, and then take a look at the Word of God. Joshua 1:8 says, "*This Book of the Law shall not depart from your mouth, but you shall meditate in it day and night, that you may observe to do according to all that is written in it. For then you will make your way prosperous, and then you will have good success.*" Do you see it? You are to keep your mind fixed on God's Word. It is a fact that the Lord created man, and the Bible is the instruction manual He has given to guide him in living life.

Consider this analogy- you have a mobile phone because almost everybody does these days. Take out that phone and look at it closely, you most likely can make calls and send messages with it. You probably use it for social media and maybe also as a flashlight. But do you realize your phone can do so much more than what you currently use it for? Many people underutilize their phones, not realizing that those devices have several potentials such as calendars, alarms, radios, TV capabilities, health features, and money-making apps, so many capacities we never tap into. Many phones even have voice command functions, yet most people are unaware of these features. Frankly, many only understand about 10% of their device's potential because they never read the manual. The manufacturer gave them instructions to help unlock everything the phones can do, yet many have never taken time to study it.

In the same way, God is the Manufacturer of human beings, and He has given us a "user manual," which is the Bible. If you don't read and apply this manual, you will never be able to unlock your full potential or achieve the success mentioned in Joshua 1:8. In Matthew 4:4, it says, "*But He answered and said, It is written, 'Man shall not live by bread alone, but by every word that proceeds from the mouth of God.'*" This means you are meant to live by God's Word, it is the manual for your life. Just as your phone has hidden abilities that could solve many difficulties you are experiencing, you also have untapped potential, skills, and power within you to overcome challenges. But if you don't study the Word of God, which reveals your purposes, you will remain stuck crying and struggling.

Psalm 1:1-3 puts it this way:

"Blessed is the man
Who walks not in the counsel of the ungodly,
Nor stands in the path of sinners,

Nor sits in the seat of the scornful;
2 But his delight is in the law of the Lord,
And in His law he meditates day and night.
3 He shall be like a tree
Planted by the rivers of water,
That brings forth its fruit in its season,
Whose leaf also shall not wither;
And whatever he does shall prosper."

As you devote yourself to studying and applying God's Word, it will shape your values, lifestyle, conduct, and priorities. You will discover and unlock more of your potential and achieve greater success even beyond your imagination, so determine today to dig into the Scriptures. Pray for revelation of who God says you are and how He has gifted you. Study diligently and carve out time to meditate on what you're learning.

- **Take Responsibility**

Bishop Oyedepo, renowned gospel minister, wisely stated, "Any type of Christianity that makes God completely responsible for your life and makes you do nothing is an irresponsible Christianity." As a believer, because you rely on miracles, there can be a temptation to just sit down, fold your hands, do nothing, and expect God to do all the work while giving you success. But that is not how it works. There is a popular misconception, especially among young people today, that living a life free from responsibilities is the key to happiness. But as a honest opinion, self-actualization and reaching your highest potential can never happen unless you rise to meet life's challenges and take responsibility.

Although responsibility is scary, it also presents opportunities to discover your gifts, refine them, and put them to great use. Here are some ways you can take responsibility: Start studying and asking yourself, “What can I do?” As Jordan Peterson, popular psychologist, states, "It is in responsibility that most people find life's meaning." Yes, it's easy to sit around waiting for someone else to come solve your problems-the only thing is that doing so will not unlock your potential. Instead, take a pen and paper, then write down at least 10 things you could do with your life. Ask yourself what you would truly love to do, what problems do you want to help solve?, etc, then, take action. It doesn't matter how much you plan; if you never act, you will just be wasting time and your potential will remain dormant. Imagine if Gideon never took action, the Israelites would have remained oppressed. Bezalel's gift would have remained meaningless if he had not taken charge after he had been given the spirit of wisdom in craftsmanship. You must be willing to work hard if you want your potential realized.

Here are some ways to take responsibility:

- Set goals and break them down into action steps.
- Focus on developing your skills and abilities.
- Be diligent and self-motivated in using your gifts.
- Hold yourself accountable to grow and improve.
- Solve problems proactively without waiting for others.
- Have the courage to step outside your comfort zone.
- Pursue mentors and learning opportunities.
- Refuse to make excuses or blame others.

You have amazing gifts within you, but it is up to you to take ownership of developing them. God will provide the power, resources, and favor, but the initiative must come from you. Rise to the challenge! Your effort will unlock blessings greater than you can imagine. It is time for you to expect destiny doors to open as you boldly take charge of your life with God's help. He desires you to live fully and become who you were created to be. Greater fulfillment, impact, and joy await those willing to embrace responsibility. Don't wait any longer - take action and discover the greatness within you!

- **Accept Who You Are**

God created you and endowed you with amazing qualities. Joseph could interpret dreams, Gideon was a mighty man of valor, Moses was a prophet, and Peter was an apostle. Some people can sing, some can write, some are poets, some are givers, and some are counselors. It's all about discovering and accepting who you are. Everyone is not meant to do the same thing in life, neither are we all meant to carry out the same assignment in life. So stop trying to copy others, be the original God designed you to be! Imagine the trouble if the apostles tried to die for our sins instead of embracing their roles. That was Jesus' purpose as we read in Isaiah 53 and Matthew 1:21. Discovering your potential involves finding your unique self and God's plan for you. 1 Corinthians 12:12-27 illustrates this by saying, *"Just as a body, though one, has many parts, but all its many parts form one body, so it is with Christ. For we were all baptized by one Spirit to form one body. The body is not made up of one part but of many. If the foot should say, 'Because I am not a hand, I do not belong to the body,' it would not for that reason stop being part of the body. God has placed each part in the body just as He wanted."*

Verse 27 sums it up by saying, "Now you are the body of Christ, and members individually." Do you see that? You are unique, you must accept who God made you to be, and to properly fulfill your role. Although becoming your true self may seem like striving for perfection, it is actually fully embracing how God designed you.

Here are some tips:

- Spend time discovering your natural strengths and interests. What energizes you?
- Don't compare yourself to others. Run your race.
- Surround yourself with affirming people who celebrate your uniqueness.
- Identify limiting thoughts that hold you back from being yourself. Replace them with truth.
- Don't let fear of judgment or failure stop you from stepping into your calling.
- Honor your God-given personality, quirks, and differences. They make you who you are.

How the Tips play out

Discover your strengths and interests: Taking personal inventory through self-reflection, personality assessments, exploring hobbies, etc., will reveal your natural talents and passions. The examples in the passage of spiritual gifts show how understanding your uniqueness helps you find your purpose.

Don't compare yourself: Comparisons are dangerous because they make us try to be something we're not. Just as every body part has its different functions, we each have a special role. Comparing stifles our ability to identify and walk in our gifts. Be confident in how God made you and who He made you to be.

Surround yourself with affirmation: Many times, we tend to internalize what others say about us. As a result of this, their words have the power to drown out the criticisms that keep us from boldly accepting ourselves. This is why you should choose friends who see the potential of greatness in you.

Identify limiting mindsets: Things like, "I'm not talented," “I am not good enough,” or "I'll never measure up" are not God's truth about you, no, these are the devil's lies. God’s Word says the opposite, His words say that we are His masterpiece (Eph 2:10)!

So, you should endeavor to replace lies with affirming scriptures and renew your mind to unlock your identity.

Overcome the fear of judgment: Stepping into your potential and purpose can be scary when others don't understand. But pleasing God is what matters most. Don't let fear of criticism or failure rob you of your destiny. God's affirmation is enough!

Embrace your personality: Uniqueness reflects God's creativity, and your personality reveals how He made you - be you an introvert, extrovert, quirky, serious, etc. Let your individuality shine and always celebrate your uniqueness because this will help you conquer mediocrity and low self-esteem.

The key idea is that God has given you a special role that only you can play. Though the world will try to squeeze you into its mold, stay true to how your Creator fashioned you. When you boldly accept your divine design, you will unlock blessings and potential you never thought possible! Stay grounded in God's love, and become who you were destined to be.

- **Dream Big but Start Small**

You won't automatically discover, unleash, and

maximize your potential overnight. More often, you will need to start small and grow into bigger things. Having big dreams is a great way to push yourself to unlock your gifts.

Whether you want to start a charity, build a house, or become a renowned singer or preacher, no matter your goal, you have to begin with humble steps. If you wait until you think you have arrived or have perfect conditions, you will never start. Yes, big dreams can feel intimidating, but you shouldn't avoid them because of fear.

You may decide you want to change the world, but where do you start? Begin right where you are, in your current position. Lofty aspirations are daunting, and fear can tremendously hinder you from becoming all God intends. The simplest solution is to break each dream down into bite-sized pieces that are easier to chew. Look at your goals again, and walk through everything needed to achieve them. As you start pursuing those dreams through small actions, your gifts will be revealed and released. You will begin to see God's supernatural abilities in you and beyond.

Here are some tips to start unlocking your potential through smaller steps:

- Pray boldly about your big dream, then listen for God's wisdom on the next step.
- Focus on improvement and progress, not perfection. Expect to fail but get back up!
- Be humble and hungry to keep growing your skills.
- Volunteer in areas related to your dreams to gain experience.
- Find a mentor who is further down the path that can guide you.
- Set short-term goals that build in the direction of your ultimate vision.
- Leverage opportunities and open doors that can help propel your dreams.

God plants purposeful desires in our hearts. But turning those dreams into reality requires persistence, courage, and faith. Don't despise small beginnings (Zech 4:10). As you are faithful with a little, God will entrust you with more. Keep taking the next step, and soon you will be further than you imagined!

Stay bold and determined as you actively develop your potential. You were created to do great things for God's glory. But it starts with a single act of obedience today. Believe in the gifts inside of you. God will get you where you need to be at just the right time.

- **Establish Excellent Habits:**

Never underestimate the power of habits. Bad ones like smoking, procrastinating, or always being late can prevent you from becoming your best self. On the other hand, good habits are the key to realizing your full potential. Doing positive things only occasionally, like exercising, eating healthy, or learning a new skill won't reap much benefit. You will need more than a couple of attempts to become the next Jimi Hendrix on guitar! However, turning positive behaviors into habits supercharges them and significantly increases your chances of success.

Here are tips for establishing habits that unlock your potential:

- Start small: Going from 0 to 60 overnight sets you up for failure. Build the habit in gradual steps.
- Attach it to an existing habit: Linking a new habit to a consistent one makes it stick better.
- Schedule it: Use your calendar to block out time for the habit. Treat it as a top priority.
- Eliminate friction: Make it as easy as possible to do the habit consistently. Remove obstacles.
- Track progress: Logging completion gives you a

sense of accomplishment and keeps you motivated.

- Reward yourself: Celebrate hitting milestones along the way. Have an accountability partner.
- Don't break the chain: At all costs, avoid missing days and breaking momentum.

With consistency over time, these positive habits will become automatic and accelerate your growth. Picture where you could be a year from now if you establish habits of reading 30 minutes a day, exercising 4 days a week, practicing your craft daily. Small steps create huge results. Start today!

- **Seek Knowledge Through Reading**

We live in an idea economy. Great works of art, music, and business are built on creative ideas. However, true creativity doesn't happen in a vacuum. We need stimulation, inspiration, and education to generate innovative ideas that help unlock our potential. And few avenues provide that better than a really good book.

The best part is that reading widely exposes you to awesome concepts regardless of genre - whether it's poetry, novels, comics, nonfiction, or anything else.

Here are the benefits of being a lifelong reader:

- Gain new perspectives that challenge your assumptions.
- Discover stories different from your own experiences.
- Explore fresh subjects and fields of knowledge.
- Encounter creative ways of expression and design.
- Find inspiration and fuel for your imagination.
- Continuously grow your skills, vocabulary, and capabilities.

If you want to maximize your potential, read daily and broadly. Great thinkers and leaders throughout history were devoted readers. The pages of a book contain worlds of insight waiting for you to explore. Unleash your inner genius - read to learn, grow, and spark new ideas!

- **Embrace Failure:**

If you want to get anywhere close to your full potential, one thing is certain - you will fail along the way. I know that's not easy to hear, but how you respond to failure is what matters most. You must view failure as an essential stepping stone on the path to success and discovering your gifts.

Although not the most pleasant thought, failure is a critical component of achievement. One of the best things you can do is accept failure openly and even embrace it each time it happens. On the journey to uncovering your potential, the road will not be smooth, but the failures are part of the process. When you stumble, get back up. When you fall down, stand again. Don't allow failure to leave you stagnant and inactive. The enemy wants you paralyzed by fear of trying new things, but you must break out of that mindset. God has placed so much within you - you need to push beyond the boundaries of failure to see it unlocked.

Here are some ways on how you can learn from failures:

- Reframe failure as feedback to fuel growth.
- Analyze what went wrong objectively and make adjustments.
- Surround yourself with encouraging people who uplift you after a setback.
- Remember failure is not your identity, it's just an event along the way.
- Allow the feelings of disappointment to motivate you, not discourage you.
- Stay confident in your abilities even if results say

otherwise.

- Trust God's purpose and timing and always know that it's not over yet!

Failure does not disqualify you, some of the most influential people experienced massive failures on their way to greatness. The only real failure is allowing a setback to terminate your progress. You have limitless potential in God's strength. Keep persevering through obstacles, and you will reach new heights!

The Key of Patience in Unlocking Your Potentials

Unlocking your full potential requires tremendous patience. Yes, it does! It was Myles Munroe who wisely said, "*Man is like an onion. His potential is exposed one layer at a time until all he is is known by all.*" What this infers is that growth is a gradual process of unveiling the gifts God has placed within you. There are no shortcuts to maturity and discovering who you were created to be. The potential within you will always demand patience. Like peeling back the layers of an onion, becoming your best self and unleashing your potential means you have to be continually shedding old mindsets, fears, and limitations. You uncover strengths, talents, and dreams at a deeper level as you push forward. This does not happen overnight, so you must be ready to persevere. There will be plateaus of progress and periods of waiting, there will be times where you may feel you have stalled, yet you must never forget that God is still at work beneath the surface, preparing you for new levels.

The temptation will be to rush or force things to happen on your own timing, but the greatest danger is for you to begin moving ahead before God's timing and prematurely exposing your inner layers. The proper timing and sequence are just as essential as the effort and intention, so allow God to determine your pace of growth and be sensitive to when He says, "wait" or "move forward."

You must never forget that developing patience also has to do with graciously accepting where you are now in life even as you work towards discovering and unleashing your potential. Appreciate the present blessings instead of being in a hurry for what's next. God is intentional about the speed of your progress to shape your character, and as you trust His timing, you will become wiser, stronger, more courageous, and more humble.

Another very necessary thing is for you to have

realistic expectations when discovering your potential. Many people want to jump from stage one of life to stage 50 - of course life doesn't work like that! You will only land yourself in trouble if you do things in such a manner. Small daily improvements are what compound over months and years to unleash your full potential and purpose. So never forget that failure and difficulties are inevitable in this path of discovering and unleashing your potential. It is persisting patiently through challenges that will forge tenacity and resilience in your heart and ultimately lead you to success.

Again, in all you do, the most important thing is to stay anchored in your identity in Christ. You are already complete in Him even if your gifts are not fully evident. Do not forget that His breadth is in you, so avoid putting your worth in worldly measures of achievement and success, instead ensure that God is the only One Who determines your value, and He says you are His beloved child, filled with His breadth, filled with His abilities, and filled with His potentials. So, rest in this truth as you walk out your potentials and giftings, step-by-step and layer by layer. There are riches to be found in you, if you allow God to chisel you into a masterpiece in His perfect timing - a timing that will help you discover your purpose with patience, joy, and hope.

Great things come to those who wait upon the Lord. Your best is yet to come!

CHAPTER 3

MAXIMIZING THE BREATH OF LIFE WITHIN YOU

"God's breath carries within it the seeds of our divine capabilities. Let's cultivate, nurture, and unleash them for His glory."

Working out The Gift of God in you

Knowing you have potential is one thing, but maximizing it and making full use of it is another. For emphasis, as long as you are breathing, you can never be empty! You did not come into this world as an empty vessel. From your mother's womb, you came with the breath of God. So, what you should do is, first, dedicate time to discover your unique abilities. What sparks joy and energy in you? Pay attention to the desires God planted in your heart as they often indicate

His purpose for you. Always be willing to experiment and try new things to unlock what you're gifted in. You should also not fail to nourish your potential through consistent growth and learning; read books, take classes, find a mentor to develop your skills, grow through failures, receive feedback with an open mind, and stay teachable with humility.

Yes, you also have to put your gifts into action through service, use them to benefit others, and solve problems; whether at church, at your workplace, or in everyday life. Step out in courage to impact the world around you, connect your abilities to God's greater Kingdom purpose, ask yourself how your gifts advance the work of His heart in the world, and let these eternal perspectives guide how you apply your potential.

God's Breath Creates Possibilities In You

As previously mentioned, everyone, everybody, every human, male or female who is breathing carries divine potentials. When God breathed life into your nostrils, He transferred some gifts and talents into you. If you are sitting there breathing in and out then it means you are an embodiment of God, created with His abilities alive in you! Never forget this, and it will be repeated until it sinks into your heart.

What an incredible truth, *"If you have breath, you have God-given talents and dreams inside of you."* When the Lord bent down and breathed into the nostrils of the first man, He imparted part of His divine makeup into every human being. His infinite creativity, wisdom, purpose, and power took up residence in our innermost being. Do not take lightly the breath in your lungs, it represents the immeasurable potential housed in your spirit. You have within you everything needed to fulfill your destiny, to make a great impact in this world, and in the life of everyone that crosses your path. Yes! The seed of greatness is there in you, life from the Source of all life and it only needs to be watered, nourished, and allowed to grow.

It's not enough to simply know you have these potentials, you must maximize it! God did not give you talents and dreams so you can live a dormant life. He intended them to be cultivated and unleashed for His glory. Just having raw potential is not the end goal. It must be maximized and applied for God's Kingdom. Now, imagine an athlete with incredible distinctive abilities but who never trains, practices, or competes. Or an inventor with brilliant ideas who never builds and tests prototypes to launch his creations - that would be very sad. You see, gifts that are not put to use always wither away over time, and you must never forget that God desires for you to be a conduit through which His power flows, not a stagnant reservoir. Beloved, it's time to maximize the breadth of life given to you! It's time to partner with the Holy Spirit and to discover your gifts; grow them through discipline and exercise them courageously. Say yes to God's call on your life by making full use of the divine potentials within you for His purposes.

God Has Given You Everything Needed

In 2 Peter 1:3, the Bible says, *"As His divine power has given to us all things that pertain to life and godliness, through the knowledge of Him who called us by glory and virtue."* What an amazing truth! Yes, this is a truth that should make you glad and shout hallelujah. By God's divine power, He has already provided you with every single thing required for living a victorious and purpose-filled life.

You do not need to strive or struggle to obtain what you need; God in His wisdom and generosity has already placed inside of you everything essential for walking in your divine calling. When He knit you together and breathed life into you, He endowed you with His supernatural gifts and talents. You entered this world thoroughly equipped and abundantly provisioned by your Creator. This means you have already been given everything needed to fulfill your destiny and maximize your potential in God. His divine power has supplied you with everything required to overcome challenges, pursue dreams, use your gifts, and make a difference in this world for eternity. The seed of greatness is within. You have all you need to bear tremendous fruit!

Some of the things God's divine power has given you:

- Wisdom greater than all human understanding
- Discernment to know His voice and truth
- Courage to step out in obedience and faith
- Strength to endure every trial and press on
- Self-control to rein in harmful desires
- Love that covers offense and seeks unity
- Hope that anchors your soul through the storms
- Perseverance and tenacity to never give up

Now let's carefully consider how each of these provisions that God has placed within you affects your potential, its maximization, and the ultimate fulfillment of your purpose and calling here on earth.

- **Wisdom greater than all human understanding**

The wisdom that God has given us in Christ far surpasses any human wisdom or intelligence. Human wisdom alone is finite and limited in perspective. But God's wisdom is all-encompassing, unlimited, and able to guide you into greater truth, purpose, and fulfillment of your potential. In 1 Corinthians 2:6-7, the Bible explains that the wisdom we have access to as believers is a "secret wisdom" - a divine mystery hidden from the world. It transcends conventional thinking or what any ruler or philosopher of this age could conceive in their limited paradigms. This wisdom enables us to grasp the depths of God's heart, plans, and desires in a way no human mind could reach through reason or study alone.

When you devote yourself to knowing Him, this supernatural wisdom takes root in you and begins to play out in your everyday decisions. It transforms how you think, evaluates situations, and makes decisions. With God's wisdom at work in your inner person, your choices and direction become aligned with His perfect will, just as if He was holding your hands and guiding every course of your life step by step. In Psalm 51:6, the Psalmist cried out saying, *"Behold, You desire truth in the*

inward parts,
And in the hidden part, You will make me to know wisdom." This verse shows that as you pray for wisdom and guidance, God will open up realities and levels of wisdom and possibilities your natural minds could never fathom or imagine. His wisdom is available to all who humbly ask God for it, as James 1:5 assures us. God longs to download His supernatural insight and paradigm-shifting ways of thinking into your spirits. When you surrender your limited perspectives to Him, the wisdom of the all-knowing, eternal God begins to guide your thoughts, words, and actions. What a glorious potential it is for you to start working with!

- **Discernment to know His voice and truth**

In addition to His wisdom, God has also imparted spiritual discernment as a potential resident in us to help us go through life and emerge as victors. The ability to distinguish truth from deception and filter out competing voices to recognize His voice above all others is a resident potential in every one of us as children of God. You see, the Bible says, *"My sheep hears my voice."* This is a potential that is available to every believer in Christ Jesus. The reference being made now is not about the gift of discernment of spirits in the book of Corinthians, but is to the potential of knowing God's will and His voice as a result of His Spirit dwelling in you. This is one potential that many people have not learned how to harness, and meanwhile, it is one of the greatest gifts that God has given to us.

Hebrews 5:14 puts it this way, "*Those who are spiritually mature have trained themselves through constant use to discern between what is righteous and what is evil.*" This discernment is ultra-sensitive to what pleases God and what goes against His heart. Jesus said in John 10:27 that His sheep listen to His voice and follow Him. Despite a thousand different voices vying for our attention daily, with discernment we can cut through the noise and clearly recognize the voice and direction of the One we love and follow. Walking in discernment allows us to use our gifts wisely, avoid potential dangers and distractions, and fulfill our purpose without compromise.

Have you ever been about to travel and somehow you just felt like you are not comfortable about the journey? That is discernment at work. Go around and make a little survey and you will discover that almost 90% of every Christian who was involved in an accident somehow felt they should not go on the journey. Somehow, they had an intuition that something wrong was going to happen but they ignored it. This is discernment!

Without a doubt, you can trace experiences in your life where this potential saved you from a lot of trouble and most likely, you have instances where ignoring this potential got you into trouble. This is a great potential that God has placed within you and you must learn to harness it or you will be cheating yourself. You need to know that you have access to the same power that raised Jesus Christ from the dead, then allow His endless divine supply of potentials within you to be uncorked and then walk in confidence that you already have everything needed because God would not give you dreams without equipping you to achieve them. Success and provision begin from the inside to the outside, and this is something you must never forget. You have everything needed to maximize your potential and live life to the fullest!

Next, consider how His Divine power has given us courage, strength, and self-control. These virtues empower us to walk in our destiny as we aim to maximize our God-given potential.

- **Courage to Step Out in Obedience and Faith**

Another privilege that you have as a result of God's Divine Power is the potential to be courageous and to step out in faith toward achieving your destiny. Sometimes the devil wants to make you feel like you are scared. He wants to fill you with doubt concerning your purpose, your potentials, your giftings, your destiny, and much more. But one thing you must realize is that fulfilling your purpose requires courage to step out boldly in obedience to God's leading and move forward in faith, even when the way seems unsure or dangerous. Yes, you really do not have to even pray for it, God's divine power has already made it available to you as a believer in Christ. here's what the Bible says in 2 Timothy 1:7:

"For God has not given us a spirit of fear, but of power and of love and of a sound mind." Do you know what this means? It means that fear is not part of what you have in God. As human beings, fear is a default response. Yet a potential you have as a result of the spirit of God in you is a potential of power, love, and a sound mind. The Spirit of God within you can override your human instincts of fear with supernatural courage and boldness.

This is evident in the early church, with the Apostles, who after being flogged and threatened, prayed for continued boldness to speak the word of God (Acts 4:29). Courage is a gift enabling us to choose faith over fear and continue advancing the Kingdom despite opposition. It takes courage to use your gift, believe in the impossible, share your faith, take risks for God, confront injustice, make unpopular stands, and live counter culturally. Many times, we often avoid these things due to fear of failure or rejection. But yielding to fear aborts destiny. What you should do is abide in Christ's perfect love which casts out fear (1 John 4:18).

The courage to step out with obedience in faith is a potential you have as a result of God's breath and spirit in you, you must begin to take active actions to intentionally act it out -maximize, work in it, and watch your life play out beautifully.

- **Strength to Endure Trials and Press On**

Inevitably, pursuing God's purpose, fulfilling destiny, and becoming great in life will bring you to a place of facing hardship and opposition every now and then. As a result of this, you must realize the need for tenacity and inner fortitude to withstand trials without vacillating or giving up prematurely. Human strength runs out quickly. But God promises us supernatural strength to endure. And this supernatural strength is something you already have as a result of His breath and spirit in you. You must learn to start walking in it, maximizing it, and using it as an advantage for your progress in life and destiny.

In Isaiah 40:31 the bible says, "*But those who wait on the Lord Shall renew their strength; They shall mount up with wings like eagles, They shall run and not be weary, They shall walk and not faint.*" This divine strength manifests when we feel we have nothing left. God's power shows up in our weakness (2 Cor 12:9).

It's important to know that as a result of God's breath and Spirit in you, you have also received perseverance and staying power sufficiently so you can outlast suffering and finish the tasks He's assigned to you (James 1:12). His strength within you is able to fuel you to keep believing when situations seem hopeless. You must rejoice in trials, forgive ongoing wrongs, and press through hardship without giving up. Yes, you can depend on this potential to renew you and sustain you during trying times. Victory is possible anyday and in every situation if you take advantage of this God-given potential in you!

- **Self-Control to Bridle Harmful Desires**

Maximizing our potentials requires keeping natural appetites and desires within proper bounds so they do not sabotage God's plan for our lives. In essence, self-control is crucial, so God in His goodness has given us supernatural self-discipline to exercise restraint and self-mastery by the Spirit. Yes, this is very true, you must stop seeing self-control as an impossible task. The more you see it as impossible, the more difficult it will be. Instead, you must realize that as a result of God's breath, and His divine power at work in you, you have the potential to control yourself. No appetite, desire, or addiction should ever be able to hold you bound and control you.

Know that the fruit which the Holy Spirit seeks to grow in you includes self-control (Galatians 5:23), and as you yield to His work on your character, He will progressively transform your passions and impulses to come under His Lordship. Even when tempted, be assured that you can resist and stand firm because of reverent devotion to God. Walking in holiness and using your gifts, talents, and potentials with integrity, require great self-restraint to avoid traps like sexual sin, addiction, dishonesty, and pride. But you can be confident that God will always provide the way of escape from temptation (1 Corinthians 10:13). Relying on Him for help builds self-control and this self-control is a provision that you already have as a result of God's breath and Spirit in you. His divine power has already made it available to you!

Pray this short prayer : "*O Lord, I look to You for daily renewal of these virtues, so that I can walk worthy of your calling and glorify You through maximizing the gifts and potential you have given me, in Jesus Mighty Name, Amen.*"

- **Love That Covers Offense and Seeks Unity**

Fulfilling our purpose and maximizing our potentials invariably has to do with dealing with people's flaws, failures, and offenses. This is inevitable in community and ministry because you are dealing with people and can expect different kinds of characters- the great and the not so great. As a result of this, you need divine love to help you overlook and cover the faults of others as well as pursue reconciliation and unity.

By now you must have found out that human love is shallow and conditional. It fails quickly when disappointed and keeps a record of wrongs, faults, crimes, and failures. But the love of the Holy Spirit which is a divine potential poured into our hearts is selfless, patient, forgiving, and perseveres through conflict. 1 Corinthians 13 describes the excellence of love that keeps no record of wrongs. It always protects, always trusts, always hopes, and always perseveres (v.7). This love empowers us to absorb offenses, let go of bitterness, and restore broken relationships. It sees the precious soul beneath every flaw.

This degree of love comes only from God as we yield our human reactions to the work of His Spirit. It enables us to walk in harmony, avoid disunity, minister in teams effectively, and bring Heaven's reconciliation to earth.

Hope That Anchors Your Soul Through Storms

Life will always bring times of uncertainty that test our hope in God, and at such times, there is a tendency for human hope to become unstable. But God's breath in us and His divine power at work in us gives us supernatural hope to anchor our souls when storms arise. This is a potential that none of us must overlook, but if you do not acknowledge that this potential is in you, then you will always look hopeless in situations and you will soon be swallowed up by depression and frustration in life.

Have you ever seen several people who go through tremendous challenges, trials, difficulties, and battles of life, and yet they never give up? They just seemed to always find the strength to continue fighting even when all odds were against them. Romans 5:5 says, *"Now hope does not disappoint, because the love of God has been poured out in our hearts by the Holy Spirit who was given to us."* This hope stabilizes us emotionally when disaster strikes, plans fail, and dreams are delayed. It lets us weep and yet cling to joy as well as rest in God's purpose beyond what we see.

Biblical hope is not wishful thinking, rather it is a confident assurance of what God will do based on His promises. This steadfast hope can help us withstand the battering waves of affliction and keep us from abandoning ship prematurely. It purifies our hearts and motivates action even when we cannot see how God will come through. Because this hope is alive within us, we can walk by faith, not sight. This hope never disappoints us in the end, because it is founded on God's proven faithfulness and not our circumstances. This is a potential and provision that God has made available to us in Christ, you have it already, it's time to believe and to start maximizing these potentials in you.

- **Perseverance and Tenacity to Never Give Up**

By His breath and divine power, God empowers us with perseverance, meaning the tenacity, ability, and potential to stand against opposition. Such a mindset makes it possible for an individual to rebuild after loss and keep pursuing divine purpose as well as his goals and destiny in spite of delays or disappointments along the way. Perseverance keeps us in the game when we want to quit early. Human stubbornness wears out quickly but the spirit of God can keep us going even in the most daring circumstances. In your study of the Bible, you will see that Jesus endured the cross. Hebrews 12:2 says that God gives us this same perseverance to withstand hardship without shrinking back. His strength manifests when ours fails.

Combined with courage, hope, and faith, the staying power God breathes in us provides and enables us to weather seasons of barrenness, rebuild after setbacks, and press on toward the upward call of God with endurance (Phil 3:14). This potential when maximized helps you to never forfeit the race prematurely, but run with tenacity until you cross the finish line.

Pray this prayer: O Lord, I praise You for these incredible provisions of love, hope, and perseverance through Your Spirit. Grant me daily renewal to walk in the fullness of these virtues and glorify You through maximizing my potentials and fulfilling Your purpose. In Jesus name, Amen!

CHAPTER 4

YOUR IDENTITY AS GOD'S MASTERPIECE

"In a world aiming to fit in, dare to stand out. Your uniqueness is your strength, your distinction and your divine fingerprint."

◆ ◆ ◆

God is Counting on You Based on Your Identity as His Masterpiece

Psalm 139:14 says, *"I will praise You, for I am fearfully and wonderfully made; Marvelous are Your works, And that my soul knows very well."* The Bible clearly declares that you are fearfully and wonderfully made. What does this mean? It means God was intentional and careful in creating you. You are a wonder, a masterpiece! You were not made casually or by chance. As a matter of fact, God designed you with precision and purpose, ensuring you were wonderfully crafted. "Wonderful" means you are loaded with potential, gifts, and talents. You are unique, special, and are an awe to the world! When you grasp this truth, you will understand why Romans 8:37 says, "*Yet in all these things we are more than conquerors through Him who loved us.*" Myles Munroe said it this way, "*You are designed by God not to blend in, but to stand out.*" Now, it's a common human behavior to want to fit in with the crowd and adopt widely accepted ways of thinking and living. But while you can learn from others, you are still one-of-a-kind, you are unique, you are one in a billion and none can actually play your role better than you. Though it's more comfortable being like everyone else, don't let the fear of standing out stop you from being fully you and who you are. Your uniqueness doesn't mean rebelling against God's principles, rather, it means embracing the distinct personality, passions, and gifts He breathed into you.

Beloved, it's so much easier to be yourself and you certainly will attract the right people too if you decide to live this way. A good advice is that you do not force yourself into society's mold when God designed you to be unique and special. Our differences as humans are by divine design, not accident. The way God made you is right and beautiful. Come to think of it, how dare the enemy tell you that you are anything less than God's masterpiece? The King of the universe created you from the depths of the earth, and you bear His creative fingerprints. He took His time, designed, formed, and then He breathed into you. Stop despising your uniqueness, and downplaying your strengths, you are made in God's image and likeness, you are a masterpiece, an original, and not a copy. Each time you fail to acknowledge your identity as God's masterpiece you are mocking God and claiming that He didn't do a good job while creating you.

God wants to showcase His artistry through people who are boldly themselves. Your distinct traits were intentional so you could fill a special gap in the world no one else can occupy quite like you. Yes, you are wonderfully made, full of potentials waiting to be unleashed and God is counting on you to be fully who He created you to be.

Reasons Never to Compromise Your Identity as God's Masterpiece

- **Only You Can Be You**

God designed each person with a unique blend of

potentials, gifts, passions, and experiences that come together to form an identity unlike anyone else. There is no one who can play your specific role in life exactly as you were meant to. When God imagined you, He had a special purpose in mind. He then crafted you meticulously with the personality, talents, and capacities to fulfill that special assignment. You were created as a masterpiece for your purpose. No one else possesses that exact mix of creativity, intellect, courage, compassion, and skill hardwired into their spirit. Even identical twins are unique individuals at their core. Trying to be like someone else forfeits the special offering only you can bring to the world. God is counting on you to be fully you, so you can fill the gap no one else was shaped for. Don't die with your song remaining unsung.

- **You Are Valuable**

When you read 1 Corinthians 12:12-27, the Bible uses an analogy of body parts working together, each carrying out their function. Just as eyes and ears have different roles, you have a special role that makes you valuable. And this special role is why God has endowed you with your own unique potential. When you compromise your identity, you become less effective.

For example, imagine your eyes trying to become the ears, their vision will then diminish. Or imagine your liver trying to become the kidney, it automatically loses its natural detoxifying abilities. In the same way, you are most valuable when operating as your true self by acknowledging your identity and the potentials that God has endowed you with. Stop trying to be someone else, instead look inward and determine the gifts and abilities that God has placed within you! You carry a glory that no one else does, the world needs you to shine your light brightly, and as you stay grounded in your identity, you will be able to give others permission to be themselves too. It is the mutual honor of our diversity that creates true beauty in the world.

- **Your Identity is Your Strength**

Fully embracing your God-given identity unlocks the access to your greatest strengths and potentials. This is because authenticity removes limitations and empowers you to operate in the gifts you were designed with. Trying to be someone else always brings frustration and stagnation because you will only find yourself struggling like a square peg in a round hole. As a matter of fact, you will find your true strengths and talents wasting away when not exercised, but in your unique identity, you are strongest, valuable, and very alive.

Sometimes, it's easy to take a look at yourself and overlook some of your gifts and talents because they seem weird, but let me encourage you right now, do not overlook traits that look quirky, idiosyncratic, or even embarrassing. Sometimes, these are the very potentials that give you an edge over everyone else. Those traits often hold the clues to your hidden greatness. In a nutshell, your identity is your superpower because God fashioned it specifically for you!

- **Fulfillment and Purpose**

It is also worthy of note that operating in your unique potentials and gifts that come with your personal identity bring tremendous joy and fulfillment. Doing so allows you to walk in your God-given purpose. The scripture in Psalm 139:14 referenced earlier says, "*I praise you because I am fearfully and wonderfully made.*" When you embrace your distinctive passions and talents, it charts the course toward purposeful work aligned with your identity. For example, when Bezalel used his artistic talents to build the Tabernacle, the Bible says God filled him with the Spirit of wisdom, understanding, knowledge, and all kinds of skills (Exodus 31:3). Using his innate gifts brought fulfillment in carrying out God's purpose.

- **Innovation and Creativity**

Boldly exercising your individuality most of the time is what unlocks and unleashes fresh innovation because God designed you to think differently. Romans 12:6 says, "*Having then gifts differing according to the grace that is given to us, let us use them: if prophecy, let us prophecy in proportion to our faith.*" Your distinct experiences breed creative solutions. For example, Esther's unique position as queen equipped her to save the Jews from genocide. Her creativity in arranging banquets for the king was the catalyst for this divine turnaround. If she had not embraced her identity, then she would have never been able to unleash her heroic creativity.

- **Resilience in Adversity**

Knowing who you are in God and your identity in him strengthens your resilience in hard times. 2 Timothy 1:7 says, "*For the Spirit God gave us does not make us timid, but gives us power, love, and self-discipline.*"

The point here is that confidence in your identity provides an unshakable foundation to weather storms. For example, when you see how Daniel clung to his convictions even under threat of death in the lions' den, you will realize that it was the strong sense of his identity in God that empowered him to stay faithful in extreme adversity. Despite pressures, if trials cannot take away your true identity in Christ, then it has no way of conquering you.

In summary, embracing the way God designed you is very vital to living out your purpose with creativity and resilience. The world needs you to be fully who you were created to be, so bring your whole authentic self out so you can thrive! Your identity is a priceless gift from The Lord. He knew the world needed exactly what He placed inside of you. That's why it's so important to never compromise the precious uniqueness He breathed into your spirit. Guard your identity as you would guard a treasure, the enemy aims to distort it through deception, shame, comparisons, and twisting your God-given passions into selfish ambition. Don't partner with anything that undermines who God declares you to be, instead you should fiercely protect your heart and the consciousness of the fact that you are uniquely created as God's masterpiece.

It will be great if you can repeat words like these to yourself every day:

- I am loved just as I am.
- I am God's masterpiece.
- I have a purpose.
- My uniqueness is beautiful.
- My gifts are irreplaceable.
- I have what it takes.

Surround yourself with people who honor your identity, and avoid relationships that pressure you to conform or perform under pressure. Most people want friends who celebrate the freedom to be who they are, so do your best to give others the same grace to walk in their identities without judgment or envy, as long as Christ is glorified.

Boldly develop your talents and passions without apology, customize your space and style to reflect your personality and I assure you that the right opportunities will celebrate diversity, not demand conformity. If something that really looks good requires you to betray your identity, then it's time to trust God to redirect you.

Have you ever heard of limiting mindsets? This is something you must break out of your life. You must break old mindsets that limit how you see yourself and how you trust your potential. Your potential is not confined to other's opinions or past labels, if God says you are anointed, powerful, and world-changing, agree with His perspective about who you are and watch your gifts explode. Take risks to express your true self, even if it draws criticism or misunderstanding, just make sure they are in line with God's demands about your life. Develop a thick skin to negative reactions because you ultimately answer to God, not man.

Over time, one will discover that a major thing that holds many people back is shame. Don't let shame abort your destiny, the only one with the right to define you is your Lord and Savior. Celebrating your God-crafted identity will release your confidence, creativity, and anointing. So no more hiding your passions and gifts, no more downplaying your strengths and uniqueness. The Lord, your Designer is proud to showcase you as His one-of-a-kind masterpiece! You are you, and that is your power. The following are some daily practices to help you maintain the consciousness of your identity as God's masterpiece:

Spend Time in God's Presence: Setting aside consistent, unrushed time to sit at Jesus' feet is vital for remembering who you are because intimacy with God realigns your perspective to see yourself as He sees you. His unconditional love will help you reaffirm to yourself that you are already accepted.

Fill Your Mind with Truth: Combat lies and false identities by constantly filling your mind with scriptural truths about who God says you are. Write them on cards and post them where You will see them often, the goal is to let these powerful reminders saturate your thinking.

Record Affirmations from God: Keep a journal of personal words, prophecies, and insightful bible verses of affirmation and scriptures God highlights for you. Review it frequently. Writing down these messages will reinforce for you your identity and self-worth as His beloved child.

Celebrate Your Uniqueness: Another vital thing is to make a list of the stand-out qualities, giftings, and passions that make you distinctly you. Revisit this often and meditate on them. Take time to thank God for the special ways He created you and refuse to take these treasures for granted.

Avoid Comparison: You will have to consciously shut out voices that reinforce false standards you should live up to. Measure yourself only by God's opinion of you. Avoid envy of others' talents and also note that comparison is the thief of contentment.

Silence Your Inner Critic: Don't partner with self-criticism, reject negative self-talk and replace it with grace. If you keep badmouthing yourself, then you are killing yourself and confidence in who God has made you to be. God convicts gently and affirms not with criticisms and condemnation, so ask Him to reverse the lens so you see yourself as He does.

Take Bold Faith-Filled Risks: Keep stepping out in areas that make you nervous and feel unqualified. This will help you build confidence in your identity and stay dependent on God's strength. You must never allow the fear of failure to stop you from daring to be who God made you.

SECTION 2:

DEALING WITH OBSTACLES

CHAPTER 5

OVERCOMING EVERY OBSTACLE

"Life's challenges aren't meant to break you; they're designed to build your resilience and strength."

◆ ◆ ◆

Understand Challenges As Part of Life

Many people realize that life on this earth is filled with difficulties and challenges. This means there will always be seasons where it feels like everything is going against you and nothing is working out according to your plans and desires. You may unexpectedly lose your job or income source; your health may take a turn for the worse just when everything seems to be going well. A relationship you cherished may suddenly develop issues, distance, or divorce. Just when you start gaining momentum toward a long-held dream, you may face a major setback, and all these could dash your hopes again and again. Life is sometimes like that - and the fact is that the Bible does not promise that there will not be challenges, but it promises that God's people will always overcome adverse situations.

In Job 14:1, the Bible says, "Man *who is* born of woman is of few days and full of trouble." The reality is that the life of a man or woman will always encounter challenges, trials, and obstacles because a broken world guarantees it.

Rather than a peaceful tranquility always, you must know that there will be days when your time on earth will be marked by pain, loss, disappointment, and uncertainty. You may experience betrayal by close friends, or you may have to bury your loved ones too soon. Your faith will be tested through the fires of adversity and sometimes, it will seem like the punches just keep coming, and you can't catch a break. Yes, there will be great times, but even after experiencing seasons of blessing, prosperity, and victory, the pendulum has a way of eventually swinging back the other way where the storms of life arise again. In essence, no bad time lasts forever nor do good times - things continually keep changing as far as life goes on.

Truly, after several years of counseling, coaching, and teaching, there is enough reason to resolve that the tests and trials of life are inevitable and unceasing. Hardship is unavoidable and no one escapes the pain and turbulence of this fallen world. Everyone's story contains chapters of intense darkness, sadness, fear, and trauma.

In a nutshell, it is true that adversity, hardship, and pain are inescapable when one is living in a broken world. They are part of everyone's experience, so don't ever get to the point where you feel like life is not fair to you, because most people have their share of the sour days. Each person's life will contain seasons of deep grief, turmoil, and disappointment, but take heart - the story is not over. God is still writing so there are bound to be better days ahead.

Let us now discuss several kinds of obstacles:

A good reason to take time to discuss these obstacles is because they are the major setbacks and challenges that many people face in life today and these obstacles are what have crippled others into thinking they are worthless, without potential, and ultimately good for nothing.

Relational Obstacles: Some of the most painful obstacles come through damaged human relationships. We feel the sting most deeply when it involves family or close friends because relationships can become strained through betrayal, bitterness, misunderstanding, or neglect over time. For example, when a close childhood friend stops investing in the friendship, they could make new friends leaving you feeling abandoned and confused. When a family member cuts you off relationally without explanation, and refuses to speak to you anymore, the rejection can crush your spirit. These relational obstacles make it hard to be vulnerable and to trust people again. You must then withdraw to avoid further pain, but shutting yourself off limits opportunities for meaningful connections, honest feedback, and relational richness. As a result, your gifts stagnate in isolation.

Circumstantial Obstacles: Another category of obstacles includes challenges arising from circumstances that are largely outside your control. For example, you experience a major injury that prevents you from doing some work you love, a natural disaster destroys part of your community, or a pandemic shuts down the economy and eliminates your industry overnight. Circumstantial obstacles can stall exciting momentums as well as make your dreams get placed on hold by forces bigger than you. Initially, it will not make sense and feel unfair but then the pain and uncertainty these situations bring sooner or later begin to paralyze a person and his or her potential.

Personal Obstacles: Some of the toughest obstacles are deeply personal ones rooted in our own limitations, weaknesses, and unhealthy patterns of thinking. Imagine being held back from taking creative risks due to paralyzing perfectionism or lack of confidence. Personal obstacles also include battling chronic illness, depression, addictions, or unresolved emotional wounds from one's past. These internal obstacles inhibit you from boldly pursuing your purpose and being all God created you to be.

Financial Obstacles: Money is frequently a significant obstacle in the life of so many people. The lack of finances can seriously limit possibilities and capacity for anyone. As an aspiring entrepreneur, for example, one may have a fantastic business idea but lack the financial capital to launch it. Picture a talented student who got accepted to her dream university but doesn't have the financial capacity to attend. Financial constraints are frustrating when you have huge dreams but little access to resources. And many times, they have a way of making one feel that the innate potentials are worthless. Insufficient finances can force you to abandon ambitions and take a "practical" path solely focused on paying bills and struggling to survive rather than actually aiming for great heights and living life to its fullest. Of course, it is a well known fact that being stuck in survival mode leaves little margin to pursue one's purpose. It is easy to put potential on hold when you're stretched financially beyond your capacity to bear.

Spiritual Obstacles: Obstacles in the spiritual realm can impact fulfilling one's potentials. For example, if you become lazy with your spiritual life, live carelessly, wallow in sin, and probably dabble into diabolical acts, this will open the door for the devil and his demons to begin putting their hands in your life. Repeatedly entertaining feelings of distance from God can also cause drifting from your purpose. How about believing lies that you have nothing to offer? This discourages using your gifts and potentials also. The enemy will always bring obstacles by tempting you to sin, addiction, isolation, pride, resentment, and other traps. But you must resist him because what he wants to do is bring a deception that obscures the truth and wears you down.

Educational Obstacles: Any time a person lacks access to quality education and training, there may be obstacles that will stop him or her from reaching their full potential. Consider a gifted mathematician who is unable to maximize her talent in an impoverished village, or an aspiring doctor who can't actualize his dream without finances for medical school. Even basic literacy could be out of reach for many because educational inequities limit their access to resources that will help develop their skills and talents. Even in such situations, one must not forget that God is able to open doors supernaturally when obstacles block the normal routes.

Government/Political Obstacles: The political climate and policies of the government can also create significant obstacles to expressing gifts and talents. For example, restrictive laws block entrepreneurs from starting innovative businesses. Sometimes, severe limitations are placed on creative arts like music, media, and literature by the government and this ends up limiting the potential of several people who are gifted in such areas. Under corrupt regimes, freedom of speech, worship, and peaceful assembly are criminalized while innocent people face persecution, discrimination, and injustice at a systemic level. These political obstacles make people shift focus to simply surviving rather than reaching for potential.

Geographic/Environmental Obstacles: Depending on where you live, environmental factors can severely limit your possibilities and potentials. Those in remote areas many times lack access to quality education, training, resources, mentors, and opportunities that urban areas provide. For example, those in lands prone to drought, natural disasters, extreme poverty, and famine are more focused on sustaining basic needs rather than maximizing potentials. They are too engrossed in their problems to think anything about their potentials, meanwhile, if they were wise they would realize that their potential has the capacity to bring them breakthroughs and success beyond imagination. Toxic pollution, contaminated water sources, and waste mismanagement all degrade health and wellbeing, resulting in a constraint to potential.

Cultural Obstacles: Components of your cultural context can inhibit the expression of your full potential, gifts, and calling. For example, gender discrimination that devalues women will limit their potentials and possibilities. Rigid cultural worldviews also ignore unique calling and gifts that don't line up with their traditional occupations and norms for acceptability. But God often calls us to break these molds for Kingdom impact because such cultural lies limit one's potential.

Overcoming the Demoralizing Power of Obstacles

As earlier discussed, life is sure to throw its share of obstacles and crises our way, it is unavoidable. But when confronted with these adversities, how you choose to respond is what makes all the difference between constructive growth and compounding tragedies that derail destiny. If met with fear, resignation, and weakness of will, the challenges you face will indeed kill the potential within you, leading to psychological scarring, withdrawn living, or worse. Now consider this story of a young elephant that was tied to a tree with a rope. At its very young and tender age, the elephant tried with all its might to break free from this constraint, but it was too small and too weak to do so. As time passed, the elephant grew into a massive, powerful creature but it had stopped attempting to break free at this time. The moral of this short narrative is that even though it eventually had the potential to easily snap out of the bonds and break free, that elephant had already been demoralized and so it stopped trying. The rope and tree represented obstacles that held the elephant back in its youth. As time passed, they succeeded in demoralizing the elephant, because even though it later had the strength to break free, it believed the obstacle was still stronger. Obstacles certainly have the power to make a person feel helpless and bound when, in fact, they have the capacity to overcome.

It is so easy to internalize thoughts such as "This is too hard" or "I'll always fail" when challenges feel non-stop. Unrelenting setbacks always try to convince us that we lack what it takes. But God has said, "Do not fear, for I am with you" (Isaiah 41:13). No matter how stuck you feel, He is right there providing the power to break through and offering encouragement. Friends, the obstacles intimidating you now cannot contain the potential God has placed inside you, so do not accept limitations. The enemy uses trials to demoralize, but God wants to strengthen your faith and reveal the abilities He has given you. Yes, you may feel too weary and battered to try again, but take heart, the battle belongs to the Lord (1 Corinthians 15:57). Victory is yours through Christ who has already overcome. His Spirit has the capacity to revive tired souls, and He is reminding you of the might and potentials you have in Him today. Rather than resignation, God is calling you to resurrection - He wants you to shake off despair and align your mind with His truth, because you are more than a conqueror. Renew your strength like the eagle, stir up the gifts He deposited deep within you, and believe in who He has created you to be. You already have everything needed to triumph over obstacles.

The mental and emotional toll of challenges will always try to cloud your identity and birthright as a child of the Most High. But break free from those lies, and refuse to allow trials to shrink who you were created to be. You have royal blood flowing through your veins. Wield your authority today to tear down strongholds of limitation. Focus on Christ and allow past setbacks to become godly setups for displaying His power in and through you. The obstacle only appears stronger, but God lives within you - and He is the true Master. Your story is just unfolding - rise up boldly, the best is yet to come!

Giants of Adversity are Stepping Stones to Destiny

When you read the story of David and Goliath, you will see that a formidable obstacle stood before Israel's path, yet it was a direct confrontation that transformed the barrier into a stepping stone toward destiny. As the soldiers of Israel assembled for battle, the towering Philistine champion, Goliath, *"stood and shouted to the ranks of Israel, 'Why have you come out to draw up for battle?'* Mocking them, his words rang out, *"I defy the armies of Israel this day; give me a man, that we may fight together."* (1 Samuel 17:8-10).

For forty days, King Saul and all in Israel's army had been dismayed and greatly afraid of Goliath. Their obstacle seemed to be unconquerable and as a result of this, all their hopes of triumph collapsed in the face of improbable victory against this intimidating symbol of trouble named Goliath. As formidable challenges often do, Goliath shook the armies' faith to its very core, compelling them to stand powerless and toothless in the valley of inaction. The Israelite's army cowered in fear of the taunting Philistine giant, Goliath. But you see, the young shepherd named David was filled with zeal for the Lord. When he asked about the reward for any man who could defeat this enemy, David's eldest brother scolded him, scoffing, who do you think you are? But David boldly declared he would speak, undeterred by insult or impossible odds. You must learn to be like David in matters such as this one- people, circumstances, and challenges will always try to derail you, but you must choose never to allow them to make you give up on your dreams and potential.

Even when he was brought before King Saul who also scorned him, David was resolute as he testified to past victories where he had defeated a lion and a bear when protecting his father's flock. With God's help established as precedent, he was assured of victory again by steadfast faith. The Bible tells us that Saul attempted to help David by giving David his armor, but the young man refused, saying he could not use those tools since he was not used to them. Shedding the false securities offered him and rather using a sling and stone, David later defeated the great adversary of God's people. We too must stand firm and never be weighed down by others' limitations and fears. An important lesson here is that David had his potential and his unique identity, and he stuck with those. Many people would have rushed to receive the King's armor, but this would be the same thing as refusing your unique identity and trying to be like someone, which in turn would have led to a definite loss in the battle. So be yourself, you don't have to copy people because God created you to be an original.

On the day of battle, rushing straight at imposing Goliath, David proclaimed, "You come with sword and spear, but I come in the name of the Lord!" Though the giant cursed him, David's focused faith destroyed Goliath with a single stone to the forehead. The weapon of trust in God and belief in his potential destroyed the mighty opponent. Through courage, boldness, and reliance on his God-given potential, David transformed an impossible obstacle into a doorway of success that he would forever enjoy all through his life.

You might be facing your own Goliaths today, it could be health diagnoses, financial disruptions, relationship issues, failures, or accidents that thwart your dreams. Are those not reasons to rise in faith by trusting the same God who sustained you before? What is adversity if it's not an opportunity for unrealized potential to emerge? Your obstacles are meant to prepare you for destinies beyond the horizon, and they are stepping stones that will grant you higher grounds. Never forget that there would have been no glory for David if he had not met an obstacle called Goliath.

In this life, when an overwhelming challenge arises, face it by trusting completely in God's power and victory. Command the stones of adversity to become weapons in your hand and you will watch obstacles become the bridge you cross into your promised land. Go ahead and declare boldly "*The Lord is my rock and my deliverer!*" because no giant can stand before you when you dwell in authority.

Seeing Setbacks as Gifts and Claiming Our God-Given Potentials

When troubles block our path, it's easy to get frustrated because sometimes we have worked so hard, and then wham! Sudden crisis begins to threaten our dreams. And then it feels like all the God-given talents within us must be squashed. But what if your struggles were meant to serve a sweeter purpose? What if the adversities actually hold hidden opportunities to uncover the greatness God breathed inside of you?

If you'd like a few strategies, below are some ways to

view obstacles so you can conquer them through your potential and emerge victorious in your God-given destiny.

- Embrace Challenges as Growth Opportunities

Life throws challenges our way, right? Now see it like this, it's like being given puzzles to solve. These challenges aren't roadblocks; they're chances for growth. Imagine them as tough teachers who make you smarter, stronger, and wiser. When you face an obstacle, remember this, "*And we know that all things work together for good to those who love God, to those who are the called according to His purpose...*" (Romans 8:28). This verse is a promise that even the hard times will produce great results if you keep your faith in the Lord. Also, when you approach obstacles with a learning mindset, they stop being scary monsters and become stepping stones. Have you seen a caterpillar turning into a butterfly? It goes through struggles inside the cocoon before spreading its wings and flying. Similarly, when you face challenges, it's like you're in that cocoon, growing and transforming. Every problem you solve and every hurdle you overcome makes you more resilient, more capable, and more ready to soar.

- Harness Your Inner Strength to Conquer

Sometimes we underestimate our own strength, but do you realize that you have a powerhouse of abilities within you! When obstacles show up, they give you a chance to discover these hidden strengths. Think of it like finding hidden treasures within yourself. Imagine that you are climbing a mountain, and each obstacle is like a rock on your path - that actually means you have climbing gear which in reality is your inner strength. It's like what the Bible says, "*I can do all things through Christ which strengtheneth me.*" (Philippians 4:13) This means that you have the strength to face anything, not because you're a superhuman, but because of the power of God's breath at work in you. So, when life throws a challenge your way, tap into that inner strength of God's divine power at work in you. Believe in yourself, and believe that you have what it takes to overcome. It might be tough, but remember, every hurdle you conquer strengthens your faith and your potential, and ultimately makes you a victor in life.

- Find Opportunities in Adversity

There's a popular phrase that is true for obstacles- "*Every dark cloud has a silver lining*" . When you face tough times, it's an opportunity in disguise, it's like the plot twist in your story that leads to something unexpectedly amazing. See it this way, sometimes a closed door isn't a dead end but rather it's a redirection. The Bible says, "*Trust in the Lord with all your heart, And lean not on your own understanding; in all your ways acknowledge Him, And He shall direct your paths.*" (Proverbs 3:5-6) This means that sometimes, even when things don't make sense if you trust in God and keep going, He'll guide you to something better. When life throws a curveball, take a moment, breathe, and look for the opportunities hidden within that challenge. Maybe it's a chance to learn something new, meet someone special, or discover a different path you hadn't considered. Remember, obstacles aren't dead ends. They're invitations for you to discover your strengths, grow, and find unexpected opportunities. Every challenge you face is a chance for you to shine brighter, grow stronger, and become the amazing person you're meant to be. So, don't let them scare you. Embrace them, conquer them, and let them shape you into the incredible individual you're becoming.

- Stay Resilient

Consider for a moment a tree in a storm- it bends with

the wind but doesn't break. You must be like that tree, swaying with challenges, but never breaking. The Bible says, "*But they that wait upon the Lord shall renew their strength; they shall mount up with wings as eagles; they shall run, and not be weary; and they shall walk, and not faint.*" (Isaiah 40:31) This verse means that when you rely on God's strength, you will find a renewed resilience to face anything. / when tough times come knocking, remind yourself that you're resilient. You have the strength to withstand storms and emerge even stronger.

- Turning Obstacles into Innovation

Have you heard the phrase, "Necessity is the mother of invention?" Well, it's true, when you face obstacles it challenges your creativity and forces you to think outside your boundaries, and then your full potential is released. It's an opportunity to think outside the box and find new ways to solve problems. Every obstacle is a chance for you to innovate, to find unique solutions, and to create something extraordinary by the use of your potential, so do not allow challenges to scare you and you will be amazed by what you can come up with!

Dealing with, and Overcoming Setbacks

The Power of Prayer

When facing difficulties, your first response should be to talk to God about it in prayer. Bring the issue sincerely to Him and ask for wisdom, strength, comfort, and help. Prayer aligns our hearts with God's truth and greater perspective during trials. Through prayer, you will gain courage knowing that God is in control. One great benefit of prayer is that we can honestly express our feelings and trust God to handle what we cannot deal with. Through a sincere prayer, you will receive grace and direction to take the next wise step. It is through prayer that we are reminded about the fact that we are not alone, but have the all-powerful God on our side! In every struggle, turn to God first in honest prayer.

Maintain a Victorious Mindset

Your mindset is one of the greatest keys to overcoming obstacles without getting stuck in discouragement. When a setback hits, it's easy to have thoughts like, "This is too hard" or "I'll never get through this," but you must reject that victim mentality. Instead, maintain faith-filled thoughts that focus on God's goodness, help, and ability to turn situations around for our good. See setbacks as temporary situations and not permanent dead ends. Have an attitude of persevering through difficulty, and view problems as opportunities for God to display His faithfulness. Don't give up, rather, ask God to renew your mindset, so you have victory over feelings of defeat. Your mindset profoundly affects your ability to thrive through tough times.

Learn From Adversity and Use Lessons Learned to Advance

When adversity strikes, take time to prayerfully reflect on what you can learn from the experience. Is there an aspect of your character that God wants to develop, or some values He'd like you to re-evaluate, prioritize and adjust? Difficulties have a way of maturing us and giving us invaluable wisdom. Also, you should reflect on any ways you could respond better next time. Let the experience make you wiser without growing bitter. Determine how to use the lesson to come back stronger and progress forward. God promises in Romans 8:28 that He works all things for our good. With His help, choose to grow through the situation. You will develop resilience and the capacity to help others going through similar struggles.

Look Inward

When facing trials, be self-reflective and look inward to assess where you may need personal growth and change. Ask God to reveal any ways you might be contributing to the problem or anywhere you may be making it worse. Humility and honesty are key for self evaluation or reflection. For example, a conflict with a friend may be a signal that you need to improve in listening and compassion. Frequently missing deadlines at work could indicate that your time management skills need more work. Don't just point fingers outwards. Take ownership of your part, make changes within, and obstacles become stepping stones.

Use Your Gifts and Potentials

View obstacles as opportunities to develop your potential, gifts, and ingenuity. Instead of avoiding difficulties, ask, "*How can I use my creativity/leadership/teaching, etc., to turn this around*?" God gave you unique talents for a reason - put them to work! Your abilities are often strengthened through adversity. It will then be advantageous to share your experience to help others facing similar struggles. Among other things you could do, you can write a book about the lessons gained, thus turning your experience into a resource for others to learn from.

Victory Is Coming

They say the darkest hour of the night comes just before dawn, so when darkness surrounds you, remember that light is coming! You may feel hopeless, but sudden breakthroughs often follow deep trials. Don't assume the battle is over until God says it's over. Persevere in faith knowing your weeping lasts only for the night, and that your circumstances will not defeat you. Declare God's promises over your life, because victory is sure, in Him!

CHAPTER 6

OVERCOMING EVERY MOUNTAIN BEFORE YOU

"The size of the mountain before you doesn't define your victory; it's the courage within you to climb that matters."

◆ ◆ ◆

You Have All You Need to Overcome

Are you facing a mountain of challenges that seem impossible to conquer? Are you at a place in your pursuits where you feel inadequate to continue, because you are being mocked? If the answer is in the affirmative, please remember that God has given you everything you need to overcome. As Jesus declared in John 16:33, "*These things I have spoken to you, that in Me you may have peace. In the world you* [a]*will have tribulation; but be of good cheer, I have overcome the world.*"

Notice Christ said even His own people will have tribulation and problems in this world- He did not say that giving your life to Him means no more trials will come. He did not say you will not have challenges, neither did He say everything will just be perfect. Some Christians falsely believe that faith results in a challenge or trouble-free life, however, that is not the promise of the Bible. Believers are only guaranteed that they will conquer when everything is concluded. What Jesus assured us is that although trouble is inevitable, we can have peace knowing He has already achieved the ultimate victory. No matter the severity of challenges you are facing, they cannot defeat you, because He who overcame death itself lives within you! His conquering power ensured victory when He arose triumphant. The enemy wants you to see only the mountain that looms large before you now. But lift up your eyes because your Deliverer has already reached the mountain top! He stands waving the banner of triumph and He's beckoning you onward and upward, therefore, take courage the battle belongs to the Lord, and He has never lost.

Once more, you already have everything needed to emerge victorious, just as David defeated Goliath against impossible odds. The God who helped you overcome the past stands ready to sustain you again and again, even today. His grace is sufficient for every trial you will ever face and as you trust in Him, you will never be put to shame. When challenges and opposition threaten to overwhelm you, remember that He who lives inside you is the One before whom every knee shall bow. His matchless strength is mightiest in your weakness. His peerless wisdom shatters human understanding and His limitless power removes any barrier that wants to stand before you! Hallelujah.

Yes, tough times will come and terrible challenges will come, but praise God because Jesus has said, "*Take heart, I have overcome the world!*" Through Christ, we can have joy and assurance of ultimate victory, no matter what we face. Jesus does not promise a life free from trials once we follow Him. What He guaranteed is that no matter the tribulations, we can overcome through His finished work. He has already conquered sin and death forever. The enemy is defeated. The final outcome is secured. Our breakthrough is guaranteed in Christ! The devil will still come at times like a flood, attacking from every side with overwhelming problems but let your mind be on what God has said, “His power in us is greater than any opposition.” We are not left helpless and through faith in Christ, His overcoming strength becomes our strength.

Perhaps you feel bombarded today and circumstances continually loom ominous and uncertain. Take heart because the victory is already yours in Jesus! Though momentary troubles feel all-consuming, keep the eternal perspective. Your life is hidden with Christ in God. You are seated with Him in the heavenlies. No earthly hardship can change your unshakable position and destiny in Him. Do not lose hope because of temporal storms. The Son of God abides within you, you have overcome because He has overcome! His invincible life flows through your veins, His breath flows through your nostrils. Do you not realize that you share in the same Spirit that raised Jesus from death itself? Beloved child of God, cease striving and know the battle is the Lord's. Your breakthrough is here!

It's time to believe and develop the unshakable confidence that the One who promised is faithful. Fix your eyes on Him, and not on the tribulations around you. Let circumstantial storms bring you to your knees in greater dependence upon His mighty arm. Declare with bold faith, "*If God is for me, who can stand against me*?" Cling to joy and hope amidst afflictions. Persevere in the knowledge that Christ has already overcome. No obstacle can thwart His purposes for you, because your breakthrough is imminent! The testing of your faith is producing a tenacity that will carry you from glory to glory.

Living Beyond Struggles and Managing

It's clear from Scripture that God did not place us on this earth simply to barely manage or survive. His plans and purposes for our lives are so much greater! Yet when people are asked how they are doing, many people respond, "Oh, we're just managing," even when things are going reasonably well. This limiting mindset is why many people now believe that getting by day-to-day is the best they can aim for. But this is not how God sees you or what He created you for. Jesus said in John 10:10, *"I have come that they may have life, and have it more abundantly."* The Lord does not want you barely hanging on, stretched thin just to maintain mediocrity. He desires you to live vibrantly and joyfully, thriving in the fullness He paid for! Being stuck in survival mode means you are not experiencing the heights God intends. If you are simply managing your health, relationships, career, or finances, then you are not at your best. God's perfect will is for you to flourish, not just survive. As Christ told His disciples, "I do not want you merely to occupy or exist. I want you to live fully until I return!"

God has deposited gifts and talents within you, just as the master in the parable gave his servants resources to invest. You have been entrusted with "pounds" of potential which you cannot afford to bury. God's command is for you to occupy, cultivate, and multiply what He has placed in you for His glory. The breath of God within you contains power, creativity, and purpose waiting to be unlocked. There are dreams, talents, and potential inside you right now longing to be discovered and expressed. You have all you need to thrive and leave a legacy. Arise today from merely existing to truly living. Allow the Spirit's wind to awaken adventure, purpose, and possibilities lying dormant. No more settling for less than God's best. You were made to shine brightly and impact lives through who He created you to be. The abundant life Jesus promised starts now - it's time to occupy!

Your Potentials and Gifts Can Overcome Mountains

Proverbs 18:16 tells us, "*A man's gift makes room for him, and brings him before kings.*" This powerful verse reveals how our God-given gifts and talents hold the key to opening doors of opportunity and connecting you with people who can help you overcome obstacles.

The "gift" referred to here represents the seed or potential God has planted within you such as your skills, your passions, and capacity for leadership, etc. All these potentials originate from Him and are meant to be used for His purposes. When you develop the gifts you have been given, they create a way forward and grant you favors you could never earn by your own effort. For instance, maybe you have a gift of compassion that drives you to care for the hurting. As you devote yourself to this, God opens doors for you to impact lives as a counselor or community leader fighting injustice. Your willingness to sharpen and exercise your gift creates new avenues. Or perhaps you have sharp business instincts and financial management abilities. As you faithfully steward these talents, God connects you with influential mentors and opportunities to shape commerce for the greater good. Your gift makes room for you.

When facing daunting obstacles, remember the gifts residing within you, because they hold the power to bring radical change. Just as David's gift with the slingshot brought him before King Saul to defeat Goliath against all odds, God wants to use your potential to take down the mountains before you.

Lean into your gifts today, maybe you have untapped potential as a writer, speaker, diplomat, researcher, creator, healer, or strategic thinker. Start developing whatever sparks passion in you, no matter how small it seems. As you devote yourself to your gift, God will open unexpected doors. Don't wait for perfect conditions to start, instead use what you have, where you are. Your gift will connect you with the right people, resources, and breaks at the right time. God's favor follows the faithful use of our gifts. You were not designed to be limited by circumstances or human credentials. The gifts inside you transcend background, education, or experience. They simply need to be discovered and honed. Be confident that your gift will make room for you just when you need it most. Stay expectant, the best opportunities often follow one's greatest obstacles. Your gifts will bring you before great men!

What To Do When it looks like things are failing

When life's mountains become very high, overwhelming, and seemingly insurmountable, these are some daily practices that should become useful if you want to win over them.

Capture your Mind and Thoughts: Begin each day with a mindfulness practice, grounding yourself in the present moment. Through meditation, deep breathing, or simply quiet meditation on the word of God, you should center your thoughts on positive outcomes and believe the best about the day. This habit will help you cultivate resilience and allow you to face the day's challenges with a calm and focused mind.

Count Your Blessings: Dedicate a few moments every morning or evening to count your blessings and even jot them down, I am talking about the things you are grateful for in life, it could be health, finance, good friends, or a happy family. You should look for the good in life rather than focus on the tragic situations. This practice helps you redirect your focus from what's lacking to what's present, promoting a positive mindset and resilience to overcome hurdles.

Goal Setting and Planning: Break down overwhelming tasks into smaller, manageable steps. Set daily goals that are in line with larger objectives. Planning helps in creating a roadmap, making daunting mountains appear more approachable when seen as a series of smaller hills to climb.

Physical Exercise: Engage in physical activity daily, even if it's a short walk or stretching routine. Exercise not only boosts physical health but also releases endorphins that elevate mood and reduce stress, providing the necessary energy to tackle challenges.

Mindset Reframing: Develop a habit of reframing negative thoughts into positive ones. When faced with a challenge, consciously change your inner dialogue. Instead of focusing on what might go wrong, emphasize the possibilities and opportunities present in the situation.

Learning and Growth: Dedicate time to learning new things each day. Whether it's reading, listening to podcasts, or taking online courses, continuous learning broadens perspectives and equips you with the knowledge and skills to face challenges with confidence.

Healthy Boundaries: Prioritize taking care of

your health, both physically, emotionally, and psychologically, and establish healthy boundaries. Ensure adequate rest, maintain a balanced diet, and allocate time for activities that bring joy and relaxation.

In the face of life's high mountains, these daily practices serve as tools in your toolkit, empowering you to tackle challenges with resilience, determination, and a positive outlook. Integrating these habits into your daily routine will help you nurture a mindset that sees obstacles as opportunities for growth and learning rather than insurmountable barriers.

CHAPTER 7

BECOMING MORE THAN A CONQUEROR

"Every obstacle faced is an opportunity to unleash the warrior within and conquer the boundaries of our potential."

Understanding Your Conquering Potentials

The dictionary defines "to conquer" as "to defeat an enemy, or to take control or possession of a foreign land." It has several synonyms such as defeat, beat, vanquish, trounce, annihilate, triumph over, be victorious over, best, get the better of, worst, bring someone to their knees, overcome, overwhelm, overpower, overthrow, subdue, subjugate, put down, quell, quash, and crush.

But true conquest is not about defeating others. It's about overcoming obstacles and limitations to become the best version of oneself. A true conqueror wages war not just against people, but against the enemies within such as fear, weakness, hatred, and ignorance. They battle to expand their potential, unlock their gifts, and light up the world. There are many inspiring examples in history of those who embodied this kind of conquest. Figures like Mahatma Gandhi overcame hatred with love and conquered an empire through non-violence. Helen Keller defeated blindness and deafness to become an author and activist. Nelson Mandela overcame decades of imprisonment to dismantle apartheid in South Africa. These people faced formidable foes, not armies on a battlefield, but the demons we all wrestle within. Self-doubt, despair, rage. Nevertheless, they persevered. Through sheer force of will, compassion, and moral courage, they transformed themselves and their societies. This is true conquest.

You may not face the same external obstacles as these historic figures, but I am sure you also face internal obstacles that hold you back from realizing your potential. On the battlefield of the mind, we fight complacency, fear, and the urge to settle for less. How can we overcome these formidable foes?

First, you must cultivate an unconquerable spirit, the faith that no obstacle can ultimately defeat you if you persist. With dogged determination and patience, you can dismantle any barrier in your way so you must nurture courage and the willingness to be vulnerable and weather hardship on the road to growth. With courage, no inner demon can withstand your light. Most of all, we must practice the power of love for ourselves, others, and life itself. Love is what illuminates our lives with meaning and connects us to an eternal source of strength. From this sacred wellspring, we gain the force to fight our battles with wisdom, ever expanding our circle of compassion.

With an unconquerable spirit, courageous heart, and the light of love, we can conquer any limitation or negativity within us. These are the keys to victory in the only battle that truly matters, the inner battle. By overcoming ourselves, we can unlock our boundless potential. We can become forceful yet peaceful warriors who conquer hate with love, ignorance with understanding, and pettiness with magnanimity.

More Than A Conqueror

Romans 8:37 says, "Yet in all these things we are more than conquerors through Him who loved us." God has given us everything needed not just to survive trials but to walk in victory! Too often as believers, we take a reactive posture, waiting for the enemy to attack before fighting back. But Scripture calls us to live proactively as more than conquerors, experiencing triumph even during hardship.

Being more than a conqueror means living victoriously day-to-day, not waiting for circumstances to overwhelm you. It means having Satan under your feet at all times. Romans 8:37-39 says that nothing can separate us from God's love, no powers, demons, present or future events. Despite what comes against us, we are assured of overwhelming victory in Christ who already conquered the grave! Right now, you may feel like a failure in the eyes of man. People may see you as someone who can never amount to anything. But God sees you as His victorious warrior! He knows the potential within you that will be unleashed as you walk boldly in your identity and calling.

You are not defined by your current trials or by voices of condemnation. You are defined by the Spirit of the

Conqueror Himself who lives in you! The same power that raised Jesus from death to life flows through your veins. The enemy is terrified of what happens when you begin to move in the authority that is yours as a child of the Most High. This is not a time to shrink back in fear or resignation, my friend. It's time to advance as an ambassador of the unshakable Kingdom you belong to. Take God at His Word "You are MORE than a conqueror!" You have already overcome because greater is He who is in you than anything that comes against you. Allow your mind to be renewed to who you are in Christ, a victor, not a victim. Let situations that used to intimidate you become opportunities for God's glory to be displayed as you confidently use the spiritual weapons He has given you. Walk into your destiny as a conqueror, commissioned to subdue darkness and release Heaven's light everywhere you go. The best is yet to come!

Receiving All We Need For A Godly Life

God has provided us with everything to live full, meaningful lives. This may seem hard to believe when life feels so difficult and unbearable. But I want you to know that God is taking you somewhere special. By the time you get there, You will look back with gratitude at the journey. The Bible teaches us that God can take a beggar, bless him, prosper him, and cause him to dine with kings and inherit eternal glory. No matter where you are now in life's journey, God is leading you somewhere amazing. As long as you nourish your spirit with the bread of God, as long as you draw breath, there is hope. Amen! Inside each of us is a divine seed, a spiritual potential planted by God. Very soon, this seed will sprout, and beautiful things will begin happening for you.

In Romans 8:31-32, the Bible asks: "What then shall we say to these things? If God *is* for us, who *can be* against us? [32] He who did not spare His own Son, but delivered Him up for us all, how shall He not with Him also freely give us all things?" If the Creator is on your side, what demon or darkness could oppose you? What hardship or heartache could conquer you? With God's strength, no enemy outside or inside can defeat you. No past pain or present turmoil can block your destiny. Maybe you feel surrounded by adversaries, people, or forces trying to stop you. Perhaps you believe life itself conspires against you. But remember this truth, if God is for you, who dares be against you? His love and power know no limits. Let your life line up with Him, and no opposition will prevail against you.

Weeping can endure for the night, but joy comes in the morning, and your morning of breakthrough is dawning. The seeds of greatness inside you cannot be snuffed out because God will not let your potential go to waste. In the wastelands of grief, lie buried treasures, gifts, talents, and dreams you are yet to unearth. A prayer now is that what is seeded within you will sprout miraculously in the mighty name of Jesus. Creativity you never knew you had will manifest in the mighty name of Jesus, and the abilities God planted in you will flourish in wondrous ways, in the mighty name of Jesus.

Above all, know this again and again, you are more than a conqueror, with Christ's strength in you, no obstacle can block your highest path. No challenge is greater than the power of God within you. Be patient, keep the faith, and nourish your spirit. Divine opportunities are coming that will use every experience, positive and painful, to propel you forward.

Stay centered in gratitude, for you have so much to be grateful for. God is redeeming your past and rewriting your future. Though storms may come, inward peace is always available. Though heartache lingers, joy will stir your soul. Though challenges arise, your spirit remains whole. Yes, you are stronger than you know, the seed of Christ is victorious in you and is transforming your weaknesses into strengths. What the enemy meant for harm; God is transforming for your good. Every hardship carries hidden blessings and every tear watering your soul will bear fruit in due season.

Keep moving forward, the door is opening, and yes, your life is unfolding from the inside out, revealing new wonders. There is so much ahead to delight in. No matter how dark the night may look, joy always comes in the morning. I declare in the name of Jesus that God is leading you into increasing victory, prosperity, and blessing. You are more than a conqueror, for the Creator lives within you, molding your character, igniting your potential, strengthening your strength, and lighting your path. All you need has been planted inside of you so go forward boldly realizing that you are abundantly provided for on this adventure called life. The best is yet to come.

Activating The Divine Power and Potentials Within You

Like Gideon, we often fail to recognize the incredible power dwelling within us. As Judges 6 recounts, Gideon was secretively threshing wheat to hide it from the oppressive Midianites. This enemy routinely plundered the Israelites' harvests and livestock, leaving them impoverished and afraid. During one wheat harvest, Gideon secretly worked to preserve some grain from the invaders' grasps. As he labored, an angel of the Lord appeared and simply watched in silence for a time. Then the angel spoke: "Mighty man of valor!" Gideon looked around in confusion, wondering who the angel could be addressing. For he felt no valor within himself, only fear. But the angel saw what Gideon could not see, I am talking about the seeds of courage and leadership buried inside him, a potential that even Gideon had failed to realize just as you have failed to realize many of God's gifts in you.

Yes, many of us are like Gideon, hiding from the enemies we perceive around us without realizing the power residing within us is far greater than anything the enemy could think of. We focus on external oppression rather than internal strength, but 1 John 4:4 says, "The One who is in you is greater than the one who is in the world." Beloved, I need you to know that within each of us is a divine power stronger than any opposition we face. When you awaken to this indwelling Spirit and boldly answer His call, no obstacle can hinder you and the world will marvel at what God can accomplish through a yielded vessel.

Gideon protested his weakness, just as we often do. He said, “I am the least in my family, my clan is small and weak.” He argued. But the angel saw beyond his excuses to the valor, leadership, and destiny dormant within Gideon. Though he felt unqualified, God saw his possibilities. The question for you is, will you choose to see yourself as God sees you, a mighty man or woman of valor or would you rather see a weakling without potentials?

Are you hiding your light under a bushel today because of fear of enemies outside? I want you to know that your true self within is far greater than any opposition, why settle for a fraction of your identity when you are a child of God? From the moment you were knit together in the womb, seeds of greatness were sown into the very being of your soul. Potentials granted by God himself are bubbling within you, waiting to be discovered.

Sometimes you need to realize that as a result of your ongoing learning and experiences, new capacities are awakening within you and hints of your destiny are constantly beckoning you to boldly emerge. Do not make excuses when God calls you to rise higher - instead, give more, risk boldly, love unconditionally, and unleash every bit of your potential without restraints. You are a unique work of art painted in the palm of God's hand so stop hiding in self-doubt, stop belittling your worth, and stop looking down on what you can accomplish as a result of God's breath within you. The same power that raised Jesus from the dead resides in you so not even death can limit you.

This very moment, determine to unlock the fullness residing in your spirit. Let the light within you permeate every aspect of your life, know that the Lord God of the universe is strengthening you from within, guiding you into blessings, and leading you from one level of triumph to another. If God is for you, who can oppose you? Child of God, no hardship can thwart your purpose or defeat you successfully in destiny, every experience is refining you, calling forth your potentials, and drawing you closer to your success. You were designed for greatness, crafted by God for a special mission. Do not minimize your abilities like Gideon. Do not fear shadows. The Holy Spirit lives in your heart and He believes in you when you do not believe in yourself. So, never forget that you are stronger than you know, wiser than you realize, and more loving than you comprehend.

Go forward boldly, mighty one, shake off hesitation, and silence self-doubt. Any limiting beliefs that once held you back will wither in the light of God's empowering truth shining from within you in the mighty name of Jesus! It's time for you to unleash the fullness seeded within you through prayer, faith, and bold actions. As you liberate your gifts and potentials you will be a blessing to the world. As you discover your true self, you will inspire others to do the same. Never forget that the obstacles on your path are strengthening your character, and preparing you for new levels of service. Challenges test your mettle but cannot limit your potential when Christ lives in you. You are becoming the courageous person of the destiny God sees which is strong, compassionate, spiritually radiant, and a world changer. Let His light and love blaze through you. Say yes to the unfolding greatness you were created to embody. Unlock the treasure chest of your soul and arise renewed, free from limitation, more than a conqueror!

CHAPTER 8

REIGNING VICTORIOUSLY IN LIFE'S BATTLES

"In every situation, seek understanding before action because wisdom lies in comprehending the battle before engaging."

◆ ◆ ◆

Understand the Situation

Although experiencing challenges every now and then is one of the guaranteed events in life, you can still live victoriously when you know how to address unwanted or unpleasant issues. Job 14:1 says that man's days are few but full of trouble, so it's no wonder that those difficulties come. How do you respond during trying times? It will be important to remember at least some principles that lead to triumph rather than defeat.

When battles arise, first seek to fully know and understand the challenge, and gather information to understand the specific situation confronting you - because the more insight you gain, the better equipped you will be to create an effective strategy. For example, don't assume a conflict with another person is about your differences. Look more deeply to grasp the other person's perspective and what unmet needs might be driving them. The more you understand the totality of what you face, the greater your chances of resolution. Sometimes you might be attacking a physical person while the real culprit behind the situation is the devil and his demons. This is why you must be careful because it's only when you understand the situation that you can truly win.

Prayerfully Develop a Plan

After you have understood the situation, the next action should be to prayerfully develop a thoughtful plan and strategy to match the battle. You see, a plan is like a road map that guides you to your destination, and no wise army ever goes to battle or conquers without a well-thought-out plan. With wisdom from God, create a step-by-step plan and approach to productively address the problem. For instance, in a conflict, how can you best communicate with the other person or persons to defuse defensiveness and build mutual understanding? What actions can turn an unhealthy dynamic into a growth opportunity? The right strategy minimizes stress and positions you for victory. If it's a financial challenge, determine where you are right now financially and also determine in clear terms where you want to be in the next three or five months, then ask yourself how you can get to where you want to be as you carefully create the solution you desire. A good plan backed up by God will always help you reign victoriously over any situation.

Trust In The Lord

Proverbs 3:5-6 says, "*Trust in the Lord with all your heart, And lean not on your own understanding; In all your ways acknowledge Him, And He shall direct your paths.*"

It is of utmost importance to remember that the ultimate victory is not in your own hands and not by your power - a lasting victory comes from God. No matter how wisely you strategize, life's battles are won by the strength of the Lord. With God, nothing is impossible, but if you fight alone, you will struggle and fail woefully because the devil is a lot smarter than any natural man. Regardless of Satan's cunningness, when you fight in line with God's unlimited and infinite power, no weapon formed against you can prosper. God wants you to do your part, then trust Him fully for the outcome of a glorious result that comes only from Him. Believers can take courage from the promise in 2 Chronicles 20:15 which says, "*The battle is not yours, but God's.*" Lift the situation up in prayer, confident that the Lord will show the way through any adversity. Yes, God is strategizing on your behalf and working all things for your growth so hold firmly in faith that His plan and purposes will prevail. You need only take each step as it is revealed in His word, trusting Him to perfect everything for you. You can rest assured that with God overseeing the bigger picture, even setbacks will produce blessings to lift you higher in the mighty name of Jesus. What first appears as a loss will become a gain, therefore focus on learning the lessons life presents, demonstrating faith and compassion each step of the way no matter how challenging. Stand firm in the truth that if God leads you into a battle, He will lead you out as a victor. Even when you feel knocked down, know that with Him, you cannot be defeated, ultimately. Your breakthrough is often just beyond the point you want to give up, so persevere with stubborn faith, because the dawn emerges after the darkest hour. Soon you will look back on the storms and see how God brought you through, stronger and wiser.

Let it always be in your mind that you were created to live fully and love boldly on this adventure called life. Difficulties will come, but God's power resides within you to transform any obstacle into growth. Listen to His voice guiding and upholding you through tests and trials, stay rooted in Him, and keep putting one foot in front of the other in faith. Go forward with courage, trusting in the victorious outcome He promises. You have survived 100 percent of your past challenges, even when you thought you couldn't bear more, and what you have endured has prepared you for this moment. God believes in you; He knows your strength and will equip you with all you need for the road ahead. You are never alone, so take hope, mighty warrior, because your greatest triumphs still await!

The Place of Your Pastor and Church As You Go Through the Battles of Life

Having the guidance of a spiritually mature pastor, and being anchored in a vibrant church assembly are invaluable for unlocking your highest possibilities and thriving in life. The truth is that a truly wise pastor always provides counsel, keeps you accountable, and nurtures your spiritual growth. Unfortunately, people often do not want to be told what to do, so they keep making blunders and ruining their lives unknowingly. Also, worthy of note is that you need to be part of a healthy church if you want to win in life and see your potential flourish. You see, a healthy church surrounds you with supportive friendships, guidance, accountability, learning, and so much more. Let's break it down in a simpler way:

First, a spiritually deep pastor who lives with integrity will mentor you in unleashing your potential. A pastor's job is to preach the truth of God's word and shepherd you, just like a true shepherd does for the sheep. Pastors will make themselves personally available to counsel you through life's complexities and decisions- when you are willing to confide in them. Their wisdom and objectivity are meant to help you reflect on what holds you back and how to align more with God's will.

When you meet a seasoned pastor, one thing you will notice is that he has walked his own journey of learning through mistakes, failures, conflicts, and inner shadows. So, it's easier for him to encourage people through trials with empathy and compassion. His maturity and scriptural knowledge have been able to make him strong during stormy days of confusion and self-doubt when he could not chart clear directions alone. So, it is very easy for him as a minister to render the same blessings to his congregation, helping them ease their pains. A pastor's guidance keeps you accountable to your highest values and potentials when you are tempted to compromise, his faith in you has the capacity to boost your own faith when you are losing hope. In essence, a pastor's role is to nurture your spiritual growth and help you unleash your God-given potential.

Beyond individual mentorship, an uplifting church assembly also catalyzes activating your highest potentials. The friendships, teachings, and group ministry opportunities the church provides will help you discover and express your God-given gifts. Serving in a church provides the opportunity to practice leadership, grow talents like music or teaching, and receive feedback to build your skills. The safe space that a healthy church offers grants you the privilege of honest sharing, allowing you to reveal your authentic self and no longer hide your struggles no matter how difficult life may look.

In church, we are joined together across differences to encourage each other's growth. The spiritual family church gives strength through all seasons of hardship and joy. The prayers uplift us; the wisdom challenges us and the teaching guides our growth in life. Overall, an uplifting church family provides a haven to unleash our best selves as we walk the path of life. The fellowship refreshes and nourishes our spirit, the teaching opens our minds and hearts, and the ministry opportunities let our light shine fully.

Some Major Pitfalls to Avoid on the Path of Winning Victoriously in Life's Battles

Becoming overly self-reliant and leaving God out: We can easily slip into trusting our own strengths and strategies more than relying on the wisdom and power of God. But self-sufficiency or a separation from God is destined for failure. As Proverbs 3:5-6 counsels, *"Trust in the Lord with all thine heart; and lean not unto thine own understanding. In all thy ways acknowledge him, and he shall direct thy paths."* Keeping God central allows you to win from the inside out.

Not knowing when to stand firm versus compromise:

Ephesians 6:13 advises to *"put on the whole armor of God, that ye may be able to withstand in the evil day."* Sometimes, it may be necessary to compromise so conflicts can be minimized. Discernment is required to know when standing firm in truth versus finding a middle ground is best. Ask God for clear guidance when facing such dilemmas.

Fighting battles in our own limited strength: When overwhelmed and fatigued, we try handling conflicts through sheer willpower. But 2 Corinthians 12:9 (KJV) promises, *"My grace is sufficient for thee: for my strength is made perfect in weakness."* Have the courage to admit when your resources are depleted because you know that His strength is made perfect in our surrender. Let God fight for you.

Falling into victimhood and self-pity: When adversity strikes, it's easy to fixate on how unfair life is and feel sorry for oneself. But this traps us in victimhood and blocks creative action. Philippians 2:14 advises, *"Do all things without complaining and disputing"*. Victimhood disempowers us when we need empowerment the most, so keep perspective through difficulties and avoid rationalizing your inaction. .

Reacting versus responding: When facing opposition or conflict, it's easy to get hooked by emotion and react from pride or fear. Proverbs 15:1 counsels "*A soft answer turns away wrath, but a harsh word stirs up anger.*" Stay grounded through prayer, and respond thoughtfully to defuse rather than inflame clashes. Reactiveness always worsens matters.

Trying to control everything: We mistakenly think controlling people and circumstances will prevent problems. But the need for control arises from fear, not true faith. Psalm 46:10 says, "*Be still, and know that I am God.*" Relax and let go of preconceived plans, then remember God's plan, not yours, wins battles.

Becoming impatient and giving up prematurely: When victory seems distant, there is a tendency to grow weary of persevering and be tempted to throw in the towel. But breakthroughs often come right after a person feels like quitting. It's no wonder that Galatians 6:9 encourages believers, stating "*Let us not become weary in doing good, for at the proper time we will reap a harvest if we do not give up.*"

Isolating: During seasons of prolonged difficulty, many people withdraw out of despair or shame about their struggles. That is one reason why we all need a loving community to rejuvenate us. "*Bear one another's burdens, and so fulfill the law of Christ.*" (Galatians 6:2) Isolating oneself makes matters worse, hence you need to allow others to comfort and strengthen you rather than stay off.

Clinging to bitterness and hurt: When conflicts or situations turn painful, some people begin to harbor resentment in their hearts. But holding onto bitterness harms us the most. "*Let all bitterness, wrath, anger, clamor, and evil speaking be put away from you, with all malice.*" (Ephesians 4:31) Practice forgiveness, even when difficult, because forgiveness is a way to remain spiritually free.

Letting fear dictate choices: Fear blurs or even blinds your perspective and has the potential to lead you into poor decisions, contrary to your values. 2 Timothy 1 verse 7 clearly says "*For the Spirit God gave us does not make us timid, but gives us power.*" That is the sufficient reason why you should wait upon God until faith arises when you are afraid.

Minimizing small wins: Many times, it is so easy to be so focused on the big goal that we overlook the little progress we are making. Every step moved forward, no matter how small, deserves celebrating. "*Let us not become weary in doing good.*" (2 Thessalonians 3:13).

With prayerful awareness, you can avoid all the pitfalls that may crop up on your path to a victorious living. When you rely fully on God's strength, remain open and flexible, and take responsibility for your mindset and actions, you are positioning yourself to go through all of life's battles wisely. Though trials come, you will avoid sabotaging yourself when they do. Believers in Christ Jesus win battles from the inside out by walking hand in hand with God, who loves His own and promises triumph over every storm!

SECTION 3

FULFILLING DESTINY

CHAPTER 9

STEPPING INTO YOUR DESTINY

"Your destiny isn't just about fame or fortune; it's about embracing the highest vision of God for your life."

◆ ◆ ◆

Understanding Destiny

"Before I formed you in the womb I knew you; Before you were born I sanctified you; I ordained you a prophet to the nations." (Jeremiah 1:5)

Have you ever asked yourself, "What should I do with my life? Why was I created? Where can my ambitions and dreams take me?" The truth is that we all wrestle with these existential questions of identity and purpose. To discover your destiny, you must begin with God, the source of revelation.

In your quiet moments of meditation, you can tap into the divine wisdom of God that knows why you have been created here on earth and explain to you what you are meant to do. God has implanted a sacred intent within each of us, a unique calling waiting to blossom. There is work only we can do, truths only our voice can speak, and light only our soul can shine. When we uncover this personal destiny and align our lives with it, we thrive. Destiny does not necessarily mean fame or fortune- for some, it may involve humble service, and for others pioneering innovation. Basically, destiny means living out the highest vision that God has placed in your hearts, and making the special contribution only you can make to the whole world. It means being who you were created to be without apology or compromise. No one else can fulfill the purpose you were designed for, and it is why you have your unique potential.

So, how do we peel back the layers and uncover this inner divine blueprint? First, you must cultivate spiritual awareness through practices such as prayer, seeking God's voice and direction, and following His instructions. In stillness, we are able to receive divine guidance not drowned out by daily noise. This is the type of guidance that only God can offer to us directly, or that He gives through the shepherd (pastor) he has placed over us.

Another thing is that you can explore your interests and potentials unapologetically, since God speaks through what gives us life and what we naturally excel at. When you feel fully alive and invest your talents in service, you will be able to line yourself up with the destiny God planned out for you. What fills your mind without struggles? What activities make time stand still for you? What brings a sense of meaning, joy, and fulfillment to your life? All these are the questions that reveal the path of destiny.

You will also gain further clarity by listening to trusted advisors who know you well. These should be those who live a life devoted to God, else you might end up going the wrong direction, not because they wanted to mislead you but because they were sincerely wrong. This is why the bible says in Proverbs 14:12, "*There is a way that seems right to a man, But its end is the way of death...*"

True ministers of God can reflect back to help find your strength, where you flourish, and where your God-given potentials shine the brightest. Wise mentors can help you interpret your soul's whispers and encourage you to walk the path of courageous self-discovery. When you tune into these channels of divine guidance, you will begin living from the inside out. Your priorities will be in line with God's intention rather than external expectations or societal pressure.

Patience and Persistence

Patience and persistence are also key in discerning God's vision and destiny for our lives. Destiny is revealed gradually, not in a lightning flash- what this means is that it continually unfolds one step at a time on a journey of faith. God calls us first to love and serve boldly where we are, not worrying about grand plans and as we remain faithful in small things, taking the next right step, our purpose crystallizes into greater assignments, calls, plans as well as giftings, then potentials unfold every day.

Sometimes destiny guides us down roads we never imagined, and what we initially desired shifts to make room for something better tailored to how God uniquely shaped us, and based on the potential he has placed in us. With prayer and openness, we begin learning to align with His divine timing, plans, and direction. When you follow these divine promptings within your heart, even without a clear blueprint, you can rest in knowing you are where you belong. You are living out God's story, not yours and you are walking in line with His will and plan for your life. As you do this patiently you will see that all the pieces of life will begin to fall into place. Passion will ignite, talents will flourish in new ways, and you will overflow with gratitude for getting to do what you were made to do.

Regardless of where you are in this journey, take heart, you were created for a divine destiny only you can fulfill. God has planted guidance within you and will reveal the next step when you are ready. For now, listen to your soul's whispers and take courageous risks to grow toward the light of what God is whispering in your spirit. By living true to who you are, you will be able to bless the world through your unique presence and potential. So, rejoice, because your purpose awaits and the journey begins from within!

CHAPTER 10

BREAKING FORTH INTO YOUR DESTINY AND KINGDOM ASSIGNMENT

"Breaking into your destiny demands breaking away from limiting mindsets and those holding you back."

◆ ◆ ◆

To break forth into your destiny is to move beyond trials, challenges, disappointments, failures, and anything else that holds you back. With your God-given potentials, you can break out of limiting mindsets and circumstances into the expansive future He has prepared for you.

In Genesis 13, we read about Abraham and Lot separating due to strife between their herdsmen. Abraham graciously gave Lot the choice of land, and

Lot chose the lush Jordan plain, leaving Canaan for his uncle. After Lot departed, God said to Abram: "*Lift your eyes now and look from the place where you are—northward, southward, eastward, and westward; for all the land which you see I give to you and your descendants forever. And I will make your descendants as the dust of the earth; so that if a man could number the dust of the earth, then your descendants also could be numbered. Arise, walk in the land through its length and its width, for I give it to you.*"

Even after his separation from Lot, Abraham's destiny was not thwarted. In fact, it would seem as though breaking away from his nephew was the pathway to breaking through into his divine destiny. Ask yourself, who are those people you need to separate from, who are those friends you need to kick out of your life, and what are those habits you need to separate from? It's time to break forth into your destiny and this means it's time to break away from them because they are limiting the launch of your potential. God expanded Abraham's vision to the limitless inheritance awaiting him, and this illustrates a key truth that with God, we can break free from any limitation that seems to box us in. A change in circumstance, relationship, or resources does not limit what God can do in the life of a willing heart.

We will all face turning points that seem like setbacks forcing us to start over at least a few times in life. If you had asked Abraham, he might not have been happy about separating from Lot, just like you may not be happy about giving up those attitudes, friends, habits, and other hindrances now. But as you remain faithful to God, He will sooner or later say, "*Arise, walk forward boldly, I have so much ahead for you.*" You see, His plans for us are not confined by current reality or circumstances, so will you choose to believe like Abraham in God's destiny being fulfilled no matter the situation? Or would you rather hold on to things you should let go of and allow them to hinder you from breaking forth into your glorious destiny and potential?

The key is to lift your eyes high above the negative, beyond the finite, into God's unlimited possibilities. When you fix your sight on God's promises rather than on your present lack, faith arises within your heart and you begin to hear God reminding you that with Him, nothing can stand in your way or thwart His purpose for your life. God has planted greatness in you waiting to emerge and His seeds of purpose are sown deep in your soul. Where you see barren ground, God says life is incubating below the surface. Stay the course, because you serve a God of multiplication and with Him, a little becomes much. He gives you just enough manna for each day so that you must rely fully on Him for provision each morning.

The advice for you right now is that you walk forward in anticipation of overflow, and trust in the God who parts seas and brings water from rocks. Do not look side to side comparing yourself to others, instead stay centered in your lane with your eyes fixed on the finish line ahead. What God spoke over you in seasons past still stands. His timeline for breakthrough is perfect, so just put one foot in front of the other and keep moving! Yes, you are called to break forth into new spiritual territory, to live from your God-given identity, not worldly labels. Heaven's counsel is for you to thrive in the deep end of faith, not cling to the shallow waters of limitation. You were born to do far more than survive, to heal, to create, and to transform. To soar up on wings like eagles, to manifest God's kingdom, and to shine your unique light. The trials you have endured have prepared you for this season of destiny. What the enemy meant to destroy you, God will use for your good and to sharpen your potential. Every experience has refined your character and fortified your faith muscles. You have emerged wiser and stronger.

God is calling you out of smallness into expansiveness, out of fear into courageous love, out of mediocrity into excellence, out of playing it safe into boldly exploring your divine potentials and gifts. This is your era to break forth into new horizons. Say yes to God's wild adventure of purpose, for at the end of your life you will not regret the risks you took in surrendering to His call. Yes, you were born for such a time as this, to live and love fully from the heart. Trust God to use every one of your talents, gifts, potentials, and experiences as seeds for miracles in this world. All He has spoken concerning your life shall come to pass, step into the destiny awaiting you, a future of freedom, favor, and transformation. The best is unfolding.

CHAPTER 11

ADVANCING FROM GLORY TO GLORY

"In moments of weakness, recall His supernatural power within you, and cling to the truth that you're destined for greatness in His time and strength."

◆ ◆ ◆

The Power of Potentials in Identifying and Overcoming Destiny Killers

As a believer, you must recognize the fact that within you lies great potentials waiting to be awakened, and that God has made incredible promises about your purpose that can lift you up whenever doubts arise. It will be great to anchor yourself in two key verses:

Joshua 1:5 declares, "*No man shall be able to stand before you all the days of your life; as I was with Moses, so I will be with you. I will not leave you nor forsake you.*" When challenges come, make a diligent effort to personalize this promise. God has said no one will oppose or thwart the destiny He has prepared for you, and it's your responsibility to know that He remains by your side through every obstacle. You are not alone and indeed can never be alone!

Isaiah 60:22 says, "*The least of you will become a thousand, the smallest a mighty nation. I am the Lord; in its time I will do this swiftly.*" Please believe that no matter how insignificant you feel, there is an exponential increase awaiting you at God's appointed time. Your human limitations cannot stop His miraculous plans, you were created to do far more than just survive, rather you are meant to unlock gifts, accomplish bold dreams, and light up the world!

Staying anchored to these promises, will empower you to withstand any storm. No matter who speaks against you, God's Word says no one can oppose His purpose for your life. No enemy can defeat you; no devil or human agent is strong enough to thwart God's plan for your life. When you feel too weak or ill-equipped, remember His supernatural power is able to work within and through you. Cling to this truth, hold tight to it, and never forget that you are destined for greatness in His time and strength. Without a doubt, there are potential destiny killers that try to hinder you from becoming who God created you to be, and recognizing these enemies is key so they cannot operate secretly.

One destiny killer is negative self-talk that breeds complacency, and this includes thoughts like "*You will never amount to much*" or "*Why even try when You will probably fail.*" Begin replacing these lies with God's empowering truth about who you are and what you're capable of in Him.

Another destiny killer to be on the lookout for is toxic relationships that reinforce limiting beliefs about yourself and what you deserve. Surround yourself instead with friends who spur you to grow, dream big, and live boldly in alignment with your values so their buoyancy can lift you higher. Destiny is also threatened when we remain in our comfort zones and refuse to take the risks required for growth. Following God's path for your life necessitates faith, courage, and vulnerability. But the other side of fear is freedom. Take a chance on yourself - you can handle more than you know.

Most of all, destiny killers operate through a root of unbelief such as doubting God's promises and power in spite of evidence to the contrary. Remembering testimonies of His past faithfulness diffuses this toxic doubt, so keep His faithfulness in your mind. He has said that you are more than a conqueror destined for great works. Will you choose to believe in Him or will you choose to wallow in doubt and unbelief?

An earnest prayer is that the forces trying to limit you will not succeed, and that God's purpose for your life will come to pass in the name of Jesus. Go ahead and release any thoughts, habits, or relationships hindering you from boldly stepping into your calling. Break free from self-imposed constraints because God has planted seeds of destiny within you that no one can snuff out. Arise, and begin unlocking your potent God-given talents and dreams. Believe in the holy path unfolding ahead. You were made for more!

Knowing Yourself to Maximize Your Potentials

Until you know yourself, you will never maximize your potential. Unlocking the gifts within you begins with a journey of self-discovery because you must be able to explore the depths of your inner world, and uncover the precious treasures buried there by God. Only by knowing your true self can you live boldly in alignment with your highest calling. Self-knowledge comes as you create space for solitude and look inward. It arrives when you listen to your own intuition that is speaking through your desires, your passions, your God-given dreams, and ambitions. You begin to know yourself as you explore your natural strengths and cast aside other people's limited expectations of who you should be. Understanding your unique personality, values, and passions is what allows you to make decisions from an authentic place.

In this process of knowing yourself, it is critical that you are honest because knowing yourself requires ruthless honesty from you. You must acknowledge your shortcomings and confront inner demons that sabotage your growth. Until you honestly extract the pains, hurts, negativity, and outer influences giving you a wrong image, you cannot walk freely. You must also acknowledge all the talents you have denied due to fear or unworthiness, knowing that each iota of weaknesses you allow will continue to hide the great strengths within you that are waiting to burst out.

True self-knowledge shapes your life journey

The better you know your gifts and what gives you

meaning, the better you can craft a purposeful life. Your calling often emerges at the intersection of your inborn talents and the world's deepest needs. But you must know yourself first before you can discern where you are most needed and how you can best serve the world through your potential.

Above all, knowing yourself allows you to live from the inside out rather than outside in. This means that you will no longer betray your values by chasing false idols, and you will stop hiding dimensions of yourself that feel unaccepted. Rather, you will be able to shed off people's expectations and boldly become who you were created to be. In other words, you are able to give voice to your authentic self, potentials, and God-given desires rather than silencing your own destiny just to favor other people.

Walking on this path of self-inquiry, and listening when your soul speaks through intuition and dreams requires courage. Reflect on moments you felt most alive, whole, and energized; and keep a journal to unpack fears, wounds, and triumphs. Surround yourself with friends who call forth your best self as you keep discovering yourself anew through each season.

Here's the truth -there is a vast landscape of gifts and potentials within you that are still uncharted and waiting to be unveiled. Do not stop your sacred journey, instead know yourself through ever-deepening layers, because it's only then can you live boldly as the person God created you to be. When you know yourself, you become unstoppable!

You Are Beyond What You Know

When you give careful thought to this idea of maximizing potential, consider how we often don't utilize the full capabilities of things we already possess, things such as cars with advanced features or iPhones with powerful technology. Most of us use only a fraction of what's already available to us, similar to how we handle our potential. God has put incredible abilities inside you, but many of those lie dormant, waiting to be awakened. Imagine if you started using even 10-20% more of what already resides in your spirit. The key is maximizing what you have, your natural talents, creativity, and capacity to hope, and dreams so be sure you make full use of the strengths and gifts you've received from God. Sometimes a person may automatically say, "*Wow, the pastor is going to teach us today how to sell stocks, how to invest in real estate, how I can get into business, how I'm going to get into whatever it is. He's going to give us the keys to how I can do that."* Partly, you are right but the goal here is not to get into any of those obvious professions and how you can do business, rather, the whole aim of this communication is to empower you to see the greatness within you. If you put any of the gains into practice you will come out on top. So, let's look at the word 'maximize', and what it stands for. When somebody asks, *"Can you define what it is to maximize?"* What might you say that word means? Well, if you look it up as a student of English or in some dictionary you will find at least a few definitions of the word, including to "make as large or as great as possible."

To maximize is to increase to the maximum. In these modern days, the vehicles we drive have a lot of features, a lot of buttons, and the likes. Most people don't even bother to figure out what those buttons are. If you are driving one of the most recent models, then you know that when you reach a certain setting, you can put it on auto-drive when driving on the highway and then you can sit down and keep your eyes on the road, and the car will continue driving itself, whether it's on a highway or a low setting. In essence, maximizing one's potential simply means using all one has been given to the ultimate possible measure.

The human potential is like an unexplored treasure trove, much like the untapped capabilities within an iPhone. How many people do you know who truly harness the entire breadth of their smartphones' functionalities? Most people limit ourselves to making calls, texting, or using social media apps like WhatsApp, Facebook, Instagram, or Snapchat. Maybe occasionally, we use it for taking pictures, but beyond these basic functions, many remain unaware of the remarkable technology embedded within these devices. The iPhone, for instance, houses an array of sophisticated features and capabilities, just like a microcosm of untapped potential waiting to be discovered.

The call to maximize your potential isn't merely a motivational slogan; it's a compelling invitation to self-introspect and unleash the latent capabilities within you. Just as we fail to explore the full spectrum of technology around us, we often fall short of exploring our own potential. This is about discovering the gifts and talents ingrained in you, and acknowledging that you possess untapped strengths and abilities waiting to be honed and utilized. Each of us harbors unique qualities, skills, and potentialities that, when acknowledged and developed, will lead to personal growth, success, and fulfillment.

The "you" that is visible to the world right now is just the tip of the iceberg. Beneath the surface, your soul is teeming with possibilities. To unlock them, you must travel the inner journey of self-discovery. Listen to your intuition and pay attention to your desires, they reveal the contours of your heart. Have the courage to explore your buried talents and shed limiting beliefs about yourself.

Practical Step to Help You Advance from Glory to Glory

- **Start your day with meditation or prayer** (at least 20-40 minutes) You set the tone for self-discovery and maximizing your potential as you begin each day with communion with the Lord and seeking His face concerning your life. Meditation calms the mind so you can hear the voice of God clearly. In a similar way, prayer helps you align yourself with God's guidance. This daily practice will help you detach from busy thoughts and create a space for fellowship with God, the only one who can truly guide your life.

- **Keep a self-examination journal**: Journaling allows you to examine your inner thoughts more deeply so set aside time to write freely about your thoughts, feelings, dreams, and challenges. Probe your experiences, relationships, and growth areas. Articulating your inner thoughts promotes self-knowledge and emotional wisdom. You should also date each entry so you can track ups and downs over time.

- **Schedule time for self-reflection:** On weekends or days off, spend quality time in self-reflection, take long walks, write in your journal, or sit in contemplative thought as you choose activities that settle your mind and help you relax without tension or anxieties. Ponder life's big questions, examine your values and priorities, and meditate on your personal desires that are pointing to your purpose.

- **Listen to your intuition**: Throughout your day, pay close attention to your heart communicating through nudges, gut feelings, and spontaneity. Your intuition is your soul's compass guiding you to the truth. This also helps you keep yourself open to God's guidance and directions; therefore, start listening before making major decisions. Your inner voice holds wisdom, your rational mind tends to miss most of the time, and you must start paying attention.

- **Learn and Grow**: Always read uplifting books, and listen to enriching podcasts or messages from sound Christian leaders. Surround yourself with wisdom that motivates personal growth and self-realization. Let these teachers inspire you to live to your highest potential.

- **Have candid conversations:** Have regular in-depth conversations with people close to you who can offer insights about your character, blind spots, talents, and possibilities for growth. Be open to their honest reflections. Those who know you well can see dimensions of yourself you may overlook, so receiving their feedback will help you build self-awareness.

- **Explore your interests:** Make time for activities you feel naturally drawn to, whether arts, sports, volunteering, or learning. As you follow your curiosity, take note of when you feel engaged, energized, and in flow. These interests and activities you gravitate to organically reveal your inbuilt talents and purpose.

- **Self Reflect:** Take 5-10 minutes before bed for self-review, and ask questions like, what brought joy today? What challenged you? Recall moments you felt grounded, loving, and authentic. Examine your emotional triggers or behavior you are not proud of and make sure you end each day growing in understanding yourself.

CHAPTER 12

HARNESSING AND GROWING YOUR POTENTIALS

◆ ◆ ◆

Discover You!

To maximize, harness, and grow your potential, you must begin by asking yourself at least a few realistic questions such as "What are my capabilities and limits? Who am I, really? What can I do? What skills do I have?,..." It is truly important to know oneself! As discussed in the previous chapter, until you know yourself deeply, you cannot fully harness the talents God placed within you. Take for example, if a billionaire suddenly gave every person in the world $1 million today. For some, this extreme blessing would lead to pitfalls, not liberation. Why? Because they do not yet know themselves, their true values, and their capacity to wisely manage such a level of blessing. But when you understand your authentic identity, you can handle any influx of blessings that come your way. You will remain grounded in purpose, channeling resources to noble ends that help others.

"Who am I?" This fundamental question often echoes in the corridors of our minds. Who are you, as an individual? It's more than just a casual inquiry; it's a deep desire to look into the depths of one's being. Understanding yourself involves unraveling the intricacies of your capacity and boundaries, and discerning the line that separates what you can achieve from what might be beyond your grasp. This knowledge of yourself is pivotal because without comprehending who you truly are, without acknowledging your strengths, limitations, and aspirations, you will find it challenging to navigate the path toward maximizing your potential. Imagine the above-mentioned scenario of an unexpected blessing, when that rich man gives everybody one billion dollars. For some, it might bring an era of prosperity and growth, a catapult towards realizing their dreams. But for others, it could signal the onset of unforeseen challenges, a destructive habit leading to personal ruin and self-destruction. This is a great reminder that not knowing yourself can lead to unintended consequences, without understanding your capabilities and limitations. Rather than being an empowerment, newfound wealth or opportunities could become a catalyst for self-destruction. If a person has known him/herself, however, the case is significantly different and will likely lead to a positive outcome. Your potential isn't just about what you can do; it's equally about recognizing what you must refrain from, what could potentially derail your path if not handled judiciously. When this knowledge is all in place you will see that wealth will become a blessing and not a curse. Jeremiah 17:9 says, "*The heart is deceitful above all things and desperately wicked: who can know it?*" Acknowledging the complexities within our hearts and minds is the first step towards self-awareness. It's recognizing the potential pitfalls that lurk within us, potentials that can either uplift or derail us.

Your Personality and Maximizing Your Potentials (A Macro or Micro)

An important aspect of maximizing your potential is in understanding whether you naturally operate with a "MACRO" or "MICRO" perspective. Some people are macro by their nature- they think big, dream boldly, and make things happen on a large scale. When pursuing goals and tackling challenges, macro individuals go for it in a gradeuse way. They have a desire to do significant, visible things that get attention and leave an impact. Contrarily, some others are micro in their personality -they prefer to operate on a small, careful scale, micro people want to handle endeavors and responsibilities in a limited, behind-the-scenes manner. They gravitate toward caution, details, and incremental progress versus bold leaps.

The truth is neither of these orientations is necessarily better than the other, both of them have their strengths, weaknesses, blessings, and potential pitfalls. Macro thinking inspires grand visions but can miss crucial details. Micro thinkers may prevent mistakes but limit opportunities. The key is knowing which tendency has the upper hand within you. Until you understand your natural macro or micro inclination, you cannot optimize your approach and maximize your gifts. Recognizing your innate perspective is essential to maximizing your potential. Entrusting a significant project to someone with a micro approach might not work well, as they prefer handling things in a smaller, cautious manner. On the other hand, someone with a macro perspective might eagerly undertake bold endeavors despite potential risks. Understanding your own approach helps in making informed decisions and taking appropriate action.

Most of the time couples exhibit opposite orientations- the husband may be macro while the wife has a micro perspective, or vice versa. This contrast can complement each other nicely if honored. But conflict arises when the husband expects his wife to initiate like him, or the wife wants her husband to be more careful in decisions. Accepting each other's nature is key. In all areas of life, take time to discern where your tendencies lie, macro or micro. At work, do you prefer generating bold ideas or refining plans? Socially, are you energized by large groups or intimate gatherings? In spiritual life, does your prayer focus on grand visions or quiet whispers? Don't automatically assume one way is better - embrace how God designed you. If you tend to be micro, accept it graciously without shame. Don't force yourself toward boldness, rather optimize your strengths for carefulness, analysis, and close connections. If you lean towards a macro personality, then channel that visionary zeal wisely by ensuring that you have micro supports e.g. meticulous team members to execute the details. Remain open to growth, but begin from self-awareness.

In Jesus' ministry, He had both micro and macro men around him. Peter was a bold initiator, while Thomas carefully analyzed. Both were necessary, and it was not in a competitive manner, because God intentionally gives the body of Christ diverse gifts that must work in harmony. If new callings require you to stretch beyond your comfort zone, do so while leaning on your natural talents. A macro leader can inspire others' gifts while empowering a micro team to execute projects. The two orientations balance each other and can be symbiotic in operations. Above all, consult God who designed you, and ask for His continuous guidance in maximizing your potentials whether macro or micro. God will expand your capacity to operate in ways you never imagined, but that begins by knowing and honoring the beautiful way He created you as an indispensable part of His body. Bring your best self, and trust Him to take care of the rest so you are exactly who He intends you to be.

How Far Do You Want to Go?

It's wise to periodically critique ourselves and assess how far we've come in life's journey. Ask yourself this question, “How satisfied am I with where I currently stand?, Is there room to grow into greater things God may have for me?” An honest self-evaluation is the key to moving from glory to glory. If your answer to the latter question is that you are content with where you are, that you've reached your goals and maximized your gifts, then blessing to you, fulfillment awaits. But if instead you admit "No, I have unfulfilled dreams and untapped potential still within," then a crucial question follows, “How far do you want to go?” You see, reaching our God-given potential requires choosing to travel much farther than we may feel prepared for or qualified to attempt. It means pursuing dreams well past our comfort zone, capabilities, and credentials. How far we reach our heights depends on how far we dare to believe. When facing great mountains like Everest, many only journey to the base camp, never venturing to scale the summit. They look up at the towering peak, and are satisfied with simply having arrived at its feet. But then, there are a select few that feel something more compelling within, an irrepressible longing to conquer the uppermost heights despite overwhelming odds, and such people cannot rest until they plant their flag on the summit!.

The question is which type are you when facing the

Everest-level challenges required to maximize your potential? Are you content with reaching the base camp and calling it a day, or does your heart burn with passion to attain the highest height regardless of the sacrifice and risk? Here's a secret, the view from Everest's peak is breathtaking, but the journey itself also changes you. Wrestling with your limits builds spiritual strength like nothing else, your character is forged, destiny is unlocked, faith is amplified and your capacity expands. When you strive towards reaching heights deemed impossible, it brings to you a holy confidence, a confidence that says within your heart, "If God brought me here, where else can He take me?" So, reader, ask yourself once more- how far do you want to go?

You see, for example, Believers in Christ all share the same eternal destination because they are born again and are all Christians. The truth however, is that their prayer lives are not the same, neither are their Word study lives, not even their service and attendance in church are the same. Do you know why? - it is because of how far each of them desires to go in their journey towards Christlikeness and a victorious life! How far each of us goes towards reaching our potential on earth depends on how relentlessly we pursue difficulty or challenge. Take it from one still on the trail, the air up ahead tastes sweeter when you exceed what you thought possible, since the sky has no limit for those who dare to climb.

So how far do you want to go, friend? Don't settle at the base camp of your potential, of your abilities, and of the success you can enjoy in this life when your Everest is still awaiting you. When you have determined how far you want to go, then you are ready for the next question.

The Next Level has a Price

After determining how far you aim to go in life, the next crucial question is "Are you willing to pay the price to get there?" Reaching your full potential requires embracing change and stepping into unfamiliar territory. Are you ready? It's easy to enjoy hearing messages about unlocking your potential and destiny while passively remaining in your comfort zone. But transformation requires getting uncomfortable, it means altering habits, priorities, and lifestyles to align with the vision God puts in your spirit. Talk must become action, so that next-level question is, "What price are you prepared to pay for the next level?"

Jesus said in Luke 14:28-30, "*For which of you, intending to build a tower, does not sit down first and count the cost, whether he has enough to finish it lest, after he has laid the foundation, and is not able to finish, all who see it begin to mock him, saying, 'This man began to build and was not able to finish?*" In other words, we must count the cost of a venture before endeavoring to maximize our potential. If a person is only willing to partially commit, never completing the mission, he will become a laughingstock stuck in mediocrity. Breakthrough requires resolute dedication to see it through, so you might want to reflect on this- what price does fulfilling your purpose require? Here are some examples:

- Sacrificing leisure priorities to devote time to mastering your craft.
- Investing finances in courses, materials, and equipment.
- Taking risks and handling rejection while pursuing opportunities.
- Persevering through setbacks and repeated failure on the way to success.
- Ignoring critics and naysayers who discourage your dreams.
- Leaving behind unsupportive relationships or

environments.

- Working harder and longer than feels comfortable.
- Stepping way outside your comfort zone repeatedly.

Maximizing potential is not passive- it takes initiative, resilience, and sacrifice. Like an elite athlete training tirelessly for the Olympics, you must be all in. When destiny calls, we either answer fully or linger in regret. I don't know your specific price, but I know that it is worth it! Don't allow fear or complacency to abort God's purposes for you. Count the cost, then boldly pay it having the understanding that with God's help, you can do all He's called you to do. Breakthrough awaits on the other side the moment you say yes to the journey ahead of you.

Embracing the Cost of Maximizing potential and fulfilling your destiny

Sacrificing leisure to master your craft: Excellence demands devoted discipline even when you are “not in the mood.” Playing video games for hours must give way to focused practice. Rather than watching shows at night, it’s time to get up early to invest time sharpening your skills and strategizing on how to get better at the things you do. You must be willing to exchange short-term fun for long-term fruit.

Investing in growth: As human beings, we spend on what we value, so are you willing to pay for classes, materials, books, conferences, and mentoring that accelerate your abilities, even if finances feel tight? View it as a seed for harvest, view it as a business investment that will definitely bring great profit, and then stay hungry and humble enough to keep learning.

Taking risks and handling rejection: Attempting great things in life and for God means repeatedly facing failure and criticism. Are you willing to share your work publicly, audition again after being passed over, or return to the drawing board? Maintain confidence in your gifts, regardless of others' reactions. Have you ever heard that the greatest risk in life is not to take any risks at all? No man ever achieved anything meaningful or great without taking risks. Every risk is worth it, yes you might not win at all, but it's better to try and fail than to sit down and regret not taking the steps at all.

Persevering through setbacks: The road to your destiny is not smooth, setbacks will definitely try your patience, perseverance, and endurance. Will you persist when progress looks hard or will you quit like a coward? You must refuse to quit when results don't manifest quickly, instead keep sowing, keep fighting, keep learning, and keep trying again and again. Victory always comes to those who outlast the battle.

Ignoring critics: Naysayers will always abound, but can you pay the price of blocking out their voices of doubt and limitation? Your calling is not up for public vote, you must realize that the only people who matter are God and those who have your best interest at heart and are ready to support you. Stay prayerful and be patient with supporters as they adjust because you answer to God alone.

Leaving unsupportive environments: There comes a point where certain relationships or environments hinder your growth. As you outgrow your surroundings, you may need to let go of what is familiar. This loneliness is temporary as God leads you to a tribe that celebrates your uniqueness.

Working outside comfort: Fulfilling purpose feels like sacrifice until your gift ignites a passion greater than comfort, so don't shy away from labor's sweat and strain. Roll up your sleeves with grateful humility then begin to work hard and work smart. This is a price you will be glad you paid in the long run of your life.

Stepping outside the comfort zone: Following Jesus always leads to unknown wildernesses that require radical trust. Are you willing to repeatedly face uncertainty and feeling out of your league? This is also another price on the path of destiny and maximizing your potentials, many times people will not understand why you make the sacrifices you are making, but that's okay, they don't have to, only wait for time and your results will explain it to them better than any of your words can ever explain.

Friend, walking in your God-given purpose and maximizing your potential is not for the timid or those with an entitlement or dependency mentality. It is for those willing to count and carry the cost, it is for the one percent of humans ready to go through discomfort and pain to sharpen their skills.

Letting Go of What Holds You Back

The "Lots" referenced here are the things that have kept you bound and stagnant all this time. The baggage you have carried that you had no business lugging around. In the Bible, the Lord called Abraham, and Abraham brought Lot with him on his journey. For a while, Lot traveled alongside Abraham, but eventually, Abraham realized that Lot was not meant to accompany him, and he said "Let us separate." Dear reader, if you do not let go of the "Lot" in your own life, you will never maximize your potential because letting go is essential for moving forward.

What is "Lot" to you as an individual? Lot represents the unhelpful habits and attitudes that weigh you down, the procrastination, the wrong relationships, the fear, the doubt, and the smallness of vision when God promises you the whole land. Lot also means you are dwelling on and clinging to past hurts and disappointments rather than stepping into your future. “Lot” is that stagnant relationship that has tied you down for years without bearing fruit. As long as you carry Lot with you, you will continue to strive and dwell in the same old ruts, unable to access the potential God has placed inside you. Letting go of Lot opens up space for you to move into all that God has for you.

In Genesis 13, Abraham finally said to Lot, "Please let there be no strife between you and me...for we are brethren. Is it not the whole land before you? Please separate from me." He told Lot to choose the left or the right, and Abraham would go the opposite way. There comes a time when you have to make a firm decision; this relationship, this habit, this attitude is not serving me so it's time to let it go. For Abraham, separating from Lot opened the door for him to step into the fullness of the promise. God blessed him abundantly once Lot was out of the picture.

Perhaps for you, it's time to let go of friends who always want something from you but never give back. Let go of relationships that seem to create more strife than joy. Let go of procrastination and plan to pursue that dream God put in your heart. Let go of past hurts and betrayals so you can love freely again. Let go of self-limiting beliefs about what you can achieve. When you let go of the wrong things, your hands are free to take hold of what God has for you. Several people who are pastors, just as an example, have faced the choice of whether to let go of some relationships and ways of operating that were holding the church back from its greatest potentials, and they can tell you, after taking some of those difficult steps of letting go, they have seen God open amazing new doors for the church. Those pastors will testify that the church would not be where it is today if they had not separated from those "Lots" that were causing strife or stagnation.

You have to personally check within yourself to see what is causing conflict and preventing you from moving forward into your purpose and potential? Declare to the attitudes, relationships, and habits that have tied you down for too long “Depart from me!” As you let go of what does not serve you, watch how God begins to open new vistas of blessing. You will find there is so much more room for the new things God wants to do, and so much more capacity to contain His promises. You have so much to offer this world. Let Lot go and walk freely into the plans God has for you!

Maximizing Your Potential by Seeing the Whole Horizon

After letting go of the "Lot" in your life, the baggage holding you back, the next vital step is gaining a whole view of the horizon. As you seek to maximize your potential, don't merely look at your current circumstances. Don't get stuck building only on where you are right now- rather, lift up your eyes, look ahead to the promises and plans God has shown you, then envision the vast vistas of possibility!

Have you ever wondered about the believers you see working hard in little corner stores and small businesses? Why is it that some folks ever so often like to play it safe, while others are taking daring risks and stepping out? The "play safe" people buy from the "risk takers" but are hesitant to start their own ventures. They fund other people's entrepreneurship but fail to courageously steward the talents God has given them. Could it be that those people are more afraid of failure than believing in God's good plans for them? The point here is that you should see the whole world and dare to conquer it because you can fully rely on God.

In Genesis 13, after Abraham separated from Lot, God told him, "*Lift up your eyes and look from the place where you are, northward and southward and eastward and westward, for all the land that you see I will give to you.*" God was revealing to Abraham the vast horizons of his destiny. Likewise, you must lift your gaze from the narrow confines of "what is" to the infinite potential of "what could be", because that is how God sees you. This discourse about maximizing your potential is because you need to know that what resides within you is far bigger than your mind can even fathom. An ongoing prayer should be that the greatness God has placed inside you will indeed come forth in the mighty Name of Jesus!

You must see beyond your current struggles and limitations and refuse to get stuck lamenting the smallness of where you find yourself today. Instead, envision the increase that is on the way. Dream big, God-sized dreams for your future and let your imagination soar! What do you see on your horizon two, three, or five years from now? Specifically, where do you envision yourself if Jesus tarries? Go ahead and close your eyes, picture it, believe it and declare "This is what I see, this is my Promised Land flowing with milk and honey... " Next, open your eyes - did you catch even a glimpse of the destiny God is calling you into? Not everyone will, for this message is not for those content with coasting through life. It is for hungry hearts yearning for more, the hearts that believe there can be more, and the hearts that know this is not the best that God intended for them.

Even if only one person catches the vision by reading this book, all heaven is cheering. Truth be told, when you get a vision, you begin seeking God's strategy to get there. You start moving in bold faith, seizing your authority, and occupying that Promised Land by advancing the kingdom step-by-step. Before long, you inspire ten more with your God-confidence, and then fifty more catch your passion. The next effect is transformation rippling through families, communities, and even nations. Never underestimate what God will do through one willing life fully surrendered to Him! Fix your gaze, and enlarge your capacity to receive God's staggering favor and blessing, because you really do not know all you are capable of, in His hands. Ephesians 3:20 puts it this way- "*Now to Him who is able to do exceedingly abundantly above all that we ask or think, according to the power that works in us.*" Dare to envision the wild dream God is breathing into your spirit. Perhaps it seems impossible in your current circumstances, but His ways and thoughts are higher. He specializes in miracles. Imagine your Promised Land, then keep stepping forward in faith, watch how He moves mountains before you and you will look back in wonder one day. Let this be your day of destiny, the day your eyes opened wide to all that God has prepared for you since before time began. Allow God to awaken faith and places inside you that you never knew existed since He sees your maximal potential. He knows every gift, skill, and talent He embedded in your soul before birth and He knows you have barely scratched the surface. But as you surrender control to Him, aligning your vision with His purposes, get ready for a venture more thrilling, more rewarding, more world-changing than you dared ask or imagine.

Launch Out!

After gaining clarity of vision and letting go of all the Lots that hold you back, the next step is to launch out! Start acting on the dream God has placed inside you. Move forward into your destiny. This then becomes the time to do your homework and prepare for liftoff, no more procrastination or hesitation. If you have been putting off pursuing that degree, then launch out and enroll in a school! If you have delayed starting that new business or project, it's time to get going on the plan and to launch out! Dig into the details, gain the skills, and make it happen! God rewards action not thoughts, so start taking steps of obedient faith. Trust Him to guide you, provide for you, and bless the work of your hands. Are you ready to launch out today? For too long, many people, even Believers have adopted a small, limited mindset when it comes to their lives and work. They clock in, earn a paycheck, pay bills...and that becomes a summary of their lives and pursuits. For such people, prayers ask no more than "God, keep me healthy so I can work next week too." Child of God, it's time to break free from small thinking! God is calling His children to begin thinking bigger, dreaming bigger, and living bigger for His glory. He wants to increase His children's capacity to contain His abundant blessings as they advance His Kingdom.

Launching out requires a bold, daring, I-will-trust-God-for-the-impossible kind of faith, and a willingness to leave behind the safe confines of what is known to pioneer something entirely new. Remember when God called Abraham to literally leave his country, kindred, and comfort zone and embark on an unknown adventure? Abraham stepped out, not knowing where He was going. This was simply because he knew God had spoken and would lead him into destiny one step at a time. Today, it is amazing to see what God did through this one life fully surrendered to His purpose. What is God whispering to you in your present moment? To start that business, write that book, invent that product, enroll in school, take a mission trip, leave that job behind? Will you launch out in radical obedience and watch what He does? With God, all things are possible as we live by faith and not fear. His purpose residing untapped within you has explosive potential to increase, bless, and influence multitudes. Say yes to the holy discontent stirring your soul. Take the limits off God and let Him show you what one life wholly devoted to Him can do. May you experience a supernatural breakthrough, provision, and blessing in all of your ventures, in the mighty name of Jesus!

After Abraham separated from Lot, God seems to have said, *"You have dwelled here in this place long enough just striving and surviving. Now get up, stretch out, and move forward claiming every promise I have spoken. Possess this expansive destiny land I am giving you!"*

Child of God, He is saying the same thing to you right now. You have been in this holding pattern too long. Now get up, get moving, and occupy every inch of Promised Land He has for you, because it is all yours! Let your capacity to dream big and receive big swell to the measure of His destiny over your life. Nothing can hold you back as you walk forward in faith, seizing your authority in Christ to prosper and increase mightily for Kingdom purpose. The Lord Himself goes before you to lead you into good success, because His promises over your life are Yes and Amen.

CHAPTER 13

WALKING IN SUPERNATURAL BREAKTHROUGH AND PROVISION

"Maximizing the gifts within you is a conduit of blessings for both you and others."

◆ ◆ ◆

Your Potentials Will Grant You Access to the Circle of Kings

It's been repeatedly emphasized that inside every person resides unique talents and abilities that are highly capable of making our world better. When you maximize the gifts God placed within you, you inevitably become a conduit of blessing. Your purpose-driven life overflows with joy and happiness, and helps to lift others' burdens. When you freely share your talents, God's light shines through you, illuminating the path for people hungry to get from where they are to where they want to be.

Just look to Biblical examples like Joseph, Esther, Deborah, and David, they were ordinary people carrying extraordinary purposes. As they surrendered their talents fully to God, unbelievable influence and impact opened up. Soon their gifts brought them right into the halls of power and policymaking, where they greatly shaped history. Solomon serves as a prime model of maximized potential attracting unimagined success. 1 Kings 10 describes the visit of the Queen of Sheba, drawn from afar by reports of His God-given wisdom and prosperity. She arrived in Jerusalem with a caravan of camels loaded with spices, gold, and precious stones to honor Solomon, and she was hardly the only dignitary to heap riches at his feet! King after king continued coming from countries near and far, eager to meet this man whose supernatural wisdom was transforming not just Israel but the known world.

Why did royalty travel for months over desert sands to seek an audience with another man? It certainly was not because Solomon pursued fame or demanded tribute as the price of sharing his gifts. Rather, the potentials God gave him created a brilliance that attracted attention from the highest levels. Excellence speaks for itself, and if you take time to maximize your potential, then nothing stands between you and kings, clients, customers, friends, and people who will ensure that your storehouse overflows with gifts, blessings, and rewards.

When you maximize your God-given talents, your light breaks forth to illuminate the world around you. Scripture promises in Isaiah 60:3 (AMP) – “*The Gentiles shall come to your light, And kings to the brightness of your rising.*" Unleash your potential, and just like Solomon, you will attract the interest of key people who can accelerate opportunities for your gifts to positively impact multitudes. It will not because you demand it, but because a generous, purposeful spirit surrounded by excellence speaks volumes.

Consider another scripture verse fromProverbs 18:16: "*A man’s gift makes room for him, And brings him before great men.*" When you maximize your talents without compromising character, God inevitably enlarges your territory. He positions you to connect with leaders who can empower your talents to transform communities, industries, and even nations. Be rest assured, leaders show up open-handed before ordinary people operating for an extraordinary purpose and that’s simply because uncommon gifts focused on helping others succeed have a magnetic effect, drawing support to advance the greater good.

According to Proverbs 22:29, "*Do you see a man who excels in his work? He will stand before kings; He will not stand before unknown men.*" A different way to communicate the same idea is that the passion and diligence you pour into developing natural talents and spiritual gifts guarantee an audience with influencers. But it's the spirit behind your efforts that sustains the interest of people in power. Are you perfecting skills for personal gain and comfort or hoping to shoulder meaningful responsibility and positively impact as many lives as possible? A selfless, service-oriented spirit focused on empowering potential in others is magnetic. And that is what truly opens doors to stand in the inner circles of kings.

My friend, take hold of the beautiful truth that you are wonderfully made, created with a purposeful potential empowered by the Lord to bless the world. No one can replicate the unique talents He has entrusted specifically to you. Allow God to awaken and direct every skill and spiritual gift within, then follow where He leads. Walk in excellence without ego or entitlement, offering back freely to Him and others what is not your own. Next, watch what opens up because every talent maximized for the good actually commands God to widely swing doors that you could never pry open yourself. Expect to attract great support drawn to the glow of what God is doing through you. Anticipate the highest levels, taking an interest in accelerating opportunities. Say yes to the journey and watch what mighty works God accomplishes as you come alive to all His purpose for you!

Unlocking Your Potential Unlocks Prosperity

As you boldly pursue the purpose for which you were created, another inevitable blessing is the attraction of material resources. When your gifts make room for you before great men and women, prosperity naturally flows your way. Those who walk in wisdom and generosity tend to have more than enough, for God Himself compels others to give to them. In Solomon's case, royalty traveled from distant lands eager to pour wealth at his feet. Year after year the parade of influential leaders continued lining up, bearing gifts of gold, silver, and precious treasures to honor this man whose supernatural wisdom was transforming not just Israel but much of the known world.

Although you may not become the richest person on earth, the truth remains that, as you maximize your talents to better the world, your needs will be met. Doors will open for your gifts to be rewarded in proportion to the problems they solve, burdens they lift, and value they add. When God positions you before those He wants to influence through you, He also moves their hearts to support the work. Are you able to imagine the future joy of paying all your bills and meeting all your needs simply by cultivating and sharing your potential? Picture shifting from barely scraping by to establishing generational wealth for your family while achieving meaningful impact. The spiritual law of sowing and reaping guarantees it because you will reap exactly where you have sown. Deuteronomy 8 puts it this way, "*If you obey God and live within His purposes, you will lack nothing.*" There will be no poor among you, so pay attention to the potentials, passions, and gifts He embedded within you. Develop talents into skills, proactively meet needs no one else can fill quite like you and doors will open for you to stand before great and mighty men and women whom heaven wants to influence through you, then the resources will come.

Keep your motives pure, not pursuing prosperity for

selfish gain, but with the aim to empower potential in others. Commit to honoring God, developing character, and living generously while building your skills. Then, stand back and watch how God brings increase because He delights in the prosperity of His servants. He makes even enemies to be at peace with you as your gifts make room for you.

Do you feel the holy discontent stirring within your heart, the desire for more meaning and impact or the longing to leave a legacy that outlasts your lifetime? Remember to start wherever you are, with whatever resources you have to develop and deploy your talents. One step leads to another when you walk in willing obedience to purpose. Before long, you will glimpse the joy, the expansion, and the abundance that naturally flows as you become who God created you to be.

CHAPTER 14

LIVING A LIFE OF SIGNS AND WONDERS

◆ ◆ ◆

Unleashing Your Gifts Makes You a Sign and Wonder

Not only does maximizing your potential open doors of success, it also causes you to shine as a sign and wonder in the world. Yes, your uncommon potentials, gifts, and talents point people to glimpse the reality of God's supernatural power operating through you!

Just look at Joseph's life for example, though brutally betrayed by jealous brothers and sold into slavery, Joseph maintained integrity and passionately developed his God-given potentials and gifts to interpret dreams and provide wise leadership. In time, he ascended in authority over Potiphar's household. Word of Joseph's uncanny abilities had eventually reached Pharaoh, who exclaimed in Genesis 41:38, *"Can we find such a one as this, a man in whom is the Spirit of God?'* Pharaoh instantly perceived that Joseph's extraordinary gifts signaled the active power of God's spirit upon him so, he immediately promoted Joseph to oversee the entire food supply during a regional famine, declaring, *"There is none so discreet and wise as you are. You shall be over my house, and all my people shall order themselves as you command."* (Gen 41:39-40)

Can you see Joseph's gifts literally transformed him into a walking sign and wonder? His leadership, wisdom, and discernment was broadcasted to all Egypt. Here is tangible evidence of the Living God actively empowering a young Israelite slave with abilities beyond the natural. What gifts rest inside of you, and what are those seemingly uncommon talents and passions waiting to be discovered and developed for a higher purpose? As you surrender your abilities to God, aligning your priorities with His Kingdom vision, get ready for a supernatural empowerment that launches you into destiny. Suddenly you will carry His glory that causes heads to turn while you exhibit a new authority, confidence, and joy that displays the reality of the Holy Spirit's presence in you. You will be able to think of solutions no one else could think of because

God's wisdom is a potential operating through you. Certainly, maximizing your gifts makes you a walking, talking, living billboard for the wonder-working God you serve! Let Him awaken your purpose and cultivate every talent with no limits from your side. As you pour it all out to advance His Kingdom, that blazing light within will become a beacon drawing hungry souls to be fed by God through you. Your anointed influence will stand as a signpost pointing the way to salvation, freedom, and the abundant life in Christ. It is true, your life can play an eternally significant part in turning the hearts of a family member, a neighbor, or even a nation back to God, but it all starts by unveiling those buried treasures and potentials, those quiet gifts resting within you. Say YES to becoming God's sign and wonder right where He has planted you, step into the journey without fear and let His Spirit's empowerment go with you.

Marks of a "Sign and Wonder" Man Unleashing His Gifts

What distinguishes the man who maximizes his God-given talents to become a walking sign and wonder? How does unleashing our potential make us living billboards of the Living God's supernatural presence and power? Consider these seven qualities blazing through a life ablaze with holy purpose.

First, he exhibits fresh confidence and authority that commands respect. Such a person will no longer hide insecurity behind mere title or position, because he carries an air of kingdom influence, speaking creative solutions and vision no one else receives. This is what then makes people inherently defer to his leadership. Second, a visible success and prosperity accompany his projects without manipulation or greed. He prospers not by scheming, but by first seeking God's purposes. The excellence he pursues simply attracts divine attention and favor since others around him take note that his fingerprints carry financial increase.

Third, this type of individuals walk in unusual wisdom beyond intellect or experience. A spiritual discernment guides their decisions to produce kingdom plunder. By routinely leaning upon the Holy Spirit's guidance surpassing natural understanding, they shine with supernatural perception decrypted from heaven's throne room. Fourth, such a man or woman demonstrates fresh joy and freedom testifying to God's goodness. While others complain or compare, they celebrate even the small breakthroughs. Gratitude gushes for doors opening, dreams being funded, and problems getting solved in undeniable response to prayer, and so their joy fuels ongoing risk-taking.

Still on the marks of signs and wonders, fifthly, a man in that category exhibits a magnetic generosity free from arrogance.He freely shares wisdom and resources, seeking no personal credit. He grasps the gifts flowing through him which originate from a surpassing Source. Thus, he stewards moments and finances with open hands, because he is compelled to empower others. Sixth, he cherishes an adventurous spirit spurred by trust in God's care and promises. The risk of failure or loss rarely deters the pursuit of the unknown. His sold-out abandonment to live by faith and not fear screams *there is a God superintending my path*! Lastly, his or her speech radiates God's love to both neighbor and enemy. While boldly proclaiming truth, little judgment or criticism colors the tone of a man or woman of signs and wonders because a tangible kindness accompanies their spiritual integrity. Seeing dignity in all people made in God's image, they lead more with empathy than condemnation.

As God awakens your purpose, cultivate these "signs and wonders' ' attitudes and dispositions because they strengthen a life aflame with surrendered gifts and fan revival. Make a personal effort to utilize the expressions of His goodness and power erupting through you, then humbly steward moments to lift the hearts of men closer to the Giver. Let all your interactions leave people remarking, "God showed up around that man, around that woman!" because you display the Spirit's reality in every word and every deed, resulting in many seeing Jesus' saving power through an ordinary life shining bright with supernatural gifts!

CHAPTER 15

ESTABLISHING YOUR GOD-GIVEN DOMINION

"Your willingness to embrace God-given potentials will lead to a supernatural acceleration of influence."

Unleashing Your Potentials Establishes God-Given Dominion

The potentials and passions inside you are so much more than mere interesting skills or abilities. They represent dominion seeds planted by the Creator, granting you authority to master a sphere of influence. When discovered and nurtured, your gifts establish God-ordained leadership no one can revoke. On the contrary, if they are ignored you forfeit the heavenly authority meant to elevate you to rule and reign.

Take one more look at examples like Joseph, Esther, and Deborah - though young and inexperienced, they cultivated their potentials and passionately nurtured talents like leadership, discernment, courage, and dream interpretation. In time, their potentials exploded in supernaturally influential ways completely out of proportion to human qualifications while their uncommon abilities thrust them into positions guiding the fate of entire nations!

Joseph's gift of interpreting dreams and administrating supply lines saved Egypt and his family from a regional famine. Esther's poised courage, beauty, and discernment reversed the Jewish genocide decree in Persia. On her part, Deborah led military campaigns to throw off the Canaanite oppression of Israel. All these people demonstrated a willingness to embrace their God-given potential and established their royal authority and leadership overnight. You must not forget that the same seeds of dominion and authority dwell within you and the skills set God infused into your personality holds clues to the areas He wants you to master, even when you have to start small. That nagging pull toward music, medicine, mechanics, writing, baking, accounting, coaching, etc. all have a message behind them. As you nurture the pull through practice and education, get ready for the supernatural wind to accelerate your influence. Before you know it, your efforts will catch the eye of a mentor, open a unique door, connect you to resources, and bring promotion. One day soon, you will glance around and realize God has established you as an authority figure influencing multitudes. This divine expansion will work not simply because you demand a position, but because nurturing your potential creates value that people are seeking, so be bold and humble, faithful in small beginnings, and say yes to the talents within you. Step into your journey without fear and watch what the God-given dominion seeds germinating in your life can yield.

Your Gifts Make You Too Blessed to Curse

Dear reader, the zeal stirring within you holds clues to the destiny God destined uniquely for you. As you explore passions, develop talents, and align your gifts with Kingdom purpose, inevitable blessing and influence open up, and then you will truly experience what it means to say that no weapon formed against one operating in God-ordained purpose can prosper!

Look at God's promise to Abraham in Genesis 12:3,

"I will bless those who bless you, And I will curse him who curses you; And in you all the families of the earth shall be blessed." When walking fully in divine will and potential, you become immune to destruction, untouchable, and shielded by Heaven because God assumes full responsibility to defend, protect, and avenge anyone who opposes His work through you. So, rather than worrying about enemies, detractors, or curses, simply focus on maximizing the seeds of greatness and potential that God planted in you. Pour yourself into nurturing your talents, stewarding resources faithfully, blessing others generously from the increasing abundance He provides, and using all of your potentials to fulfill His goals. Stay ready to bless families, communities, and even nations impacted by the gifts flowing through you. Then be rest assured that God Himself will handle any threats against you because he has said that "N*o weapon formed against you shall prosper, and every tongue which rises against you in judgment you shall condemn."* (Isaiah 54:17) You see, you dwell secure in His pavilion, hidden in the secret place of the Most High. No curse can touch you as you boldly pursue His purpose to bless the world. Even bitter people trying to curse you will end up unwillingly blessing you instead!

Think about other examples like Joseph and David, two young men who were destined by God for leadership, yet both of them were initially betrayed and cursed by those closest to them. Joseph's brothers conspired to murder him before selling him into slavery, while King Saul obsessively tried killing David out of a jealous insecurity. But heaven's decree predestined both men's journeys and no human power could veto God's sovereign plans. In fact, the enemy's attacks against them turned out to further their divine destiny! At age 30, Joseph emerged overnight as Egypt's Prime Minister after interpreting Pharaoh's dreams, strategically leading the nation and even his broken family through seven years of famine. Before his story was over, a lowly shepherd, David, ascended Israel's throne as the greatest king in history, a pioneer of worship, and an inspiration for generations.

The same goes for that purpose and destiny stirring within you! It comes with bulletproof blessing and supernatural favor woven through every fiber of your being. Yes, pursue it cautiously with wisdom, integrity, and care for people in line with God's intention. But fear no risk or barrier because no rejection, accusation, or plot against you can ultimately derail Heaven's decrees. You are too blessed to be cursed! Move forward confidently into all God has prepared for you. Your responsibility is to say yes to His call, take hands off outcomes, and watch how He establishes you blessing multitudes!

Beware Of Entitlement Mentality As Heaven Backs You

As you boldly nurture your talents and align with God's purposes, divine blessing and favor will escalate rapidly, but beware of stumbling into common pitfalls that erode integrity and limit fruitfulness. Consider the following principles that have enabled others to prevail:

Remain humble, not arrogant: All skills, wisdom or success come from the Giver through you, not innately from you. So, your assignment is to steward increasing opportunities and resources faithfully and always remain eager to return all glory to God. Self-celebration and boasting as though success came through personal greatness rather than heaven's undeserved grace will lead a person to a path of self-destruction.

Remain a passionate student: Be quick to acknowledge

how much you still don't know, and never forget that nothing shuts down learning faster than pride and pretense that a subject has been mastered when there is still much to learn. Instead, there is value in retaining a beginner's posture through lifelong learning, noting that it is growing and understanding that keeps one teachable and authentic.

Gratitude: Stay grateful by freely sharing credit and rewards with those God sends alongside to work with you. This is because Kingdom dreams become reality through partnership, not by solo efforts, and, generosity multiplies joy while jealous hoarding of fame breeds isolation and limitation.

Patience: Remain patient giving critics and doubters time and space to process information about. Do not allow anyone's opinions to derail you from the assignment God has placed on your life. Not everyone recognizes a God-given dream when it's still a seed.

Do not pretend: Freely admit weaknesses and limitations rather than pretending and giving everyone a false sense of perfection. This builds trust and a good relationship between you and others. This level of transparency will also allow God's strength to shine brighter through your fragile humanity and it will compel witnesses to credit God.

Keep Growing: Continually nurture intimacy with God above productivity and success. Make loving Him your supreme priority, not crowns or the accolades your gifts may attract.

CONCLUSION

YOU WERE CREATED FULL & DESIGNED FOR SIGNIFICANCE

One truth you must cement deeply in your spirit is that you were created by God with great value, purpose, and unlimited potential. You are not a random, empty vessel, but a masterpiece filled with His supernatural gifts and talents.

Genesis 1:27 says that God made humanity in His own image, so we possess the imprint of the divine, created to reflect God's creativity, compassion, wisdom, and power in the world. Mankind indeed originates from the workshop of the Most High, and according to Ephesians 2:10, "*We are God's handiwork, created in Christ Jesus to do good works, which God prepared in advance for us to do.*" God has gifted each of us distinctly with the potential to fulfill a unique Kingdom mission. From the foundations of time and earth, He envisioned the good works you would accomplish and deposited seeds of destiny within you, including your talents, passions, leadership, artistry, and the like.

You were not an afterthought or accident of the universe. You were conceived in the heart of God. He wired you deliberately with all you need to complete your purpose and bring Him glory. Even when you feel ordinary or ill-equipped, remember that the same Spirit who raised Jesus from death Himself lives in you! You have unlimited potential. This eternal truth destroys any lies that say you are worthless, inadequate, or without anything meaningful to offer in this world. When Satan whispers, "You will never amount to anything," God thunders, "You are my priceless child in whom I am well pleased!" You are loaded with greatness, so release the fullness of God within you. God is unlocking the strength, skills, and gifts you didn't know you had. As Creator of the universe, He breathed value into your life, so you are not empty- rather, you are overflowing with divine potential!

You are meant to fulfill divine assignments through words of hope, acts of service, overcoming battles, or an inner healing from past pains. You are endowed with leadership influence, a creativity that moves culture, and perseverance that inspires, so say yes to your calling and potential so your light shines in a world that seems to be filled with darkness!

Parting Words

The lifestyle of unleashing your full divine potentials begins and ends with faith - faith in the incredible greatness God planted inside you. Throughout this book, we have looked deep into the obstacles that keep us small and uncovered pathways to live boldly from our supernatural identity. It however takes a childlike faith to awaken to one's God-given talents. It may mean seeing with eyes of wonder and refusing to see any form of limitations that want to hold you back. You must choose each day to believe in possibilities beyond what the outer world says is realistic or prudent. If your calling beckons on you to walk on water, you will need to leave the comfort of shore behind before you see the ground rise up to meet your feet. But first, you must get out of the boat of complacency and of playing it safe according to man's rules. Take God at His word, the same word which says you were made for more than just fitting in and surviving and which confirms that you have the capacity to thrive, inspire and transform.

Don't ever forget that His breath is in you, and that He has given you all that you need to excel in this life, so let nothing or noone hold you back. Take the leap, and follow the whisper of your spirit, even when friends and family do not understand because they cannot see the vision God embedded in your heart. You must still persevere because your results will explain to them far better than your word can do the explanations. When everything is concluded, the divinely implanted dream is meant for you alone to fulfill, and it is your gift to offer to the world. You need not figure everything out first or wait for the conditions to be perfect, you only need to act on what God has spoken to you in the secret place and follow the compass of your spirit. Get moving, and God will illuminate each next step, while the path will reveal itself under your feet. You just must start now and not procrastinate any longer because this is your moment and heaven cheers you on!

It is certain that every talent you require has already been planted within and every gift you need to fulfill your purpose is already in you. You are not alone in this awakening, several others are on a similar journey and each individual unfolds according to God's timing and grace. Some seasons will test you, asking you to let go of your trust in God, but He promises that if you commit your gifts, He will direct your paths, breathe wind beneath your wings, and nourish your soul with exactly what is needed to soar. It is time to rejoice that you get to participate in this wondrous dance called life -lift up your eyes to see the abundant blessings surrounding you, and feel the joy angels have when you courageously use your potential to fulfill God's call.

As you close this book, remember that this is not the end, it is only the beginning of a new chapter in your life - a chapter of glory, lifting, and of using your potential to bless the world in yieldedness to God.

Thank you for reading, God bless you and increase you in the mighty name of Jesus.

4 DAYS WORKBOOK TO HELP YOU DISCOVER AND UNLEASH YOUR POTENTIALS

There are 10 questions allocated to each day, take time to sit down with a pen and a journal, meditate on each question, ponder them deeply, and sincerely write down your answer in a way that makes it possible to review it again. Let the questions and answers be a guide to help you as you strive toward discovering your potentials and unleashing them.

Day 1

1. What unique talents and gifts did God give you at birth? How can you nurture those innate strengths?
2. What brings your spirit alive with passion and purpose? What desires point to your soul's calling?
3. How can you create more stillness and space for self-reflection in your daily life?
4. What beliefs about yourself may be limiting you from boldly pursuing your dreams?
5. How can you expand your thinking from "either/or" limitations to empowering "both/and" possibilities?
6. What next step can you take today to act on the

visions God has placed in your heart?

7. How will accomplishing your biggest goals help and serve others?
8. What is one area where you can have greater faith in God's miraculous power operating through you?
9. How can you see current challenges as opportunities to strengthen you for your destiny?
10. What spiritual practices (prayer, affirmation, meditation) renew you and reveal guidance?

Day 2

1. Who can you connect with to gain insights into your blind spots and potentials?
2. What self-limiting habits or relationships may need releasing so your gifts can flourish?
3. How willing are you to courageously risk failure and discomfort in order to grow?
4. What inspires and re-ignites your passion when you feel like giving up?
5. How can you use setbacks or delays as growth lessons to expand your capacities?
6. What helps you maintain perspective when life feels mundane and routine?
7. How can you actively nourish your body, mind, and

emotions to handle greater responsibility?

8. Where do you see God supernaturally working through or guiding you lately?
9. How can you keep your vision fresh while also living fully in each day?
10. What does a life of stepping fully into your divine potential look like for you?

Day 3

1. What passionate interests have sparked my curiosity since childhood? What talents or skills came naturally when I pursued them?
2. What brokenness in the world arouses holy frustration in me? What solutions have I imagined to address it?
3. What connections or conversations fill me with unusual joy or energy? Do they reveal overlooked opportunities?
4. If I imagined my life's work knowing I could not fail, what would I attempt for God? What intimidates me from pursuing it?
5. What topics do people often ask my advice about? Do these point to wisdom or experience I could develop to help more people?

6. When I picture myself 10 years from now, what specifically do I see myself doing? How does that align with who God shaped me to be?
7. What past successes and accomplishments fill me with confidence I could repeat? Do they indicate latent talents I could further nurture?
8. If I could learn one new skill or ability without difficulty or cost, what would I choose and why?
9. Who has spoken an encouraging word over my life? What did they see in me I have not yet recognized in myself?
10. What connections, resources, or education would accelerate my development if I boldly asked for help? Who specifically could guide me?

Day 4

1. What habits or mindsets block me from nurturing talents and passions buried within? What first step can I take this week to shift course?
2. If money and time were no constraint, how would I actively develop my talents to help others?
3. Am I willing to leave my comfort zone to pursue God's destiny, even if my efforts initially disappoint? Why or why not?

4. What smaller steps and milestones could I celebrate as progress toward the larger vision God has shown me?
5. Who has achieved success in an area I am skilled in but hesitant to seriously pursue? Can I ask them for wisdom and advice?
6. Have I allowed past mistakes, regrets, or limiting messages from others to incorrectly define what I can achieve through faith in Christ? Why?
7. Am I willing to take regular risks pursuing God-given talents without guaranteed outcomes, trusting Him to guide me?
8. What talents and experiences have I consistently undervalued in myself that could empower others if openly shared?
9. Who specifically will benefit as I boldly develop latent talents and abilities seeded in me? How can this impact inspire action?
10. What is one intentional commitment I will make this week toward nurturing my gifts to walk in God-given destiny?

REFERENCES

Munroe, M. (2009). *Unleash Your Purpose.* Destiny Image Publishers.

Motivated2Inspire. (Feb. 19, 2021) 10 Myles Munroe Quotes on a Life Maximized. *Motivated2Inspire.* https://motivated2inspire.com/100-myles-munroe-quotes-on-a-life-of-maximized-potential/

https://www.biblegateway.com/versions/King-James-Version-KJV-Bible/

ABOUT THE BOOK

Within you lies a brilliant light waiting to shine, seeds of destiny planted by God, potentials waiting to be awakened, and sacred purposes ready to be unleashed. This book is a clarion call to step boldly into your highest potentials. Stop playing small, and stop waiting for permission. This moment beckons you to take a leap of faith into the grandest version of yourself. Discover the eternal gift only you were sent to deliver to this world. Say yes to love, joy, and a meaningful life waiting to flow through an open heart. Let today be the day you finally dare to unlock the full force of the Spirit of God that's alive within you!

Made in the USA
Middletown, DE
16 November 2024